Trusting God to Keep His Promises

In this, Margaret Jensen's seventh book, you will find hope for your times of heartache.

Through her heartwarming stories, "America's favorite Christian storyteller" recounts the painful disappointments she has experienced . . . and the peace she has found through obedience and surrender to God's will.

She trusted His promises, and the blessings came. Lives were changed. Wayward young people came home to God and became His servants. And as Margaret continues to trust, the blessings continue to come.

In *Stories by the Sea,* you will be encouraged to trust God's promises in the midst of your own heartache and disappointments.

Other books by Margaret Jensen

STORIES BY THE SEA

Trusting God to Keep His Promises

Margaret Jensen

Here's Life Publishers

First Printing, October 1990

Published by
HERE'S LIFE PUBLISHERS, INC.
P. O. Box 1576
San Bernardino, CA 92402

Printed by Dickinson Press, Inc.,
    Grand Rapids, Michigan

Cover design and illustration by Cornerstone Graphics

Library of Congress Cataloging-in-Publication Data
Jensen, Margaret T. (Margaret Tweten), 1916-
    Stories by the sea : trusting God to keep his promises / Margaret Jensen.
            p.   cm.
    ISBN 0-89840-288-3
    1. Meditations. 2. Jensen, Margaret T. (Margaret Tweten). I.
Title.
BV4832.2.J464   1990
242 – dc20   90-41693
                                                  CIP

Scripture quotations are from the *King James Version*.

For More Information, Write:

L.I.F.E. – P.O. Box A399, Sydney South 2000, Australia
Campus Crusade for Christ of Canada – Box 300, Vancouver, B.C., V6C 2X3, Canada
Campus Crusade for Christ – Pearl Assurance House, 4 Temple Row, Birmingham,
    B2 5HG, England
Lay Institute for Evangelism – P.O. Box 8786, Auckland 3, New Zealand
Campus Crusade for Christ – P.O. Box 240, Raffles City Post Office, Singapore 9117
Great Commission Movement of Nigeria – P.O. Box 500, Jos, Plateau State Nigeria,
    West Africa
Campus Crusade for Christ International – Arrowhead Springs, San Bernardino,
    CA 92414, U.S.A.

Dedicated to our son, Ralph, who turned his heart toward home — and to God.

Because of that choice, God gave him Christine Fisher, a gift of love to Ralph and all the family.

Because of their choices, many found their way to our home. We took them "as is." God made them "as His."

Twenty years later, we tell the stories by the sea.

CONTENTS

SPECIAL THANKS

With special thanks, as always, to Harold who patiently prays for the gift of interpretation as he transfers all my writings from the yellow pads to the typewriter.

Once again, I thank my special family at Here's Life Publishers, especially Jean Bryant, Barbara Sherrill, Dan Benson, Michelle Treiber, Les Stobbe, and all the rest of that dedicated team who take part in getting my books out.

Thank you, Jan and Jud Carlberg for your continued encouragement, and for standing true to God since childhood. What a miracle of God's grace!

My special love and thanks to the grandchildren: Heather and Chad Carlberg, Shawn, Eric, Sarah and Kathryn Jensen. They not only supply me with stories, but they also keep my priorities in line.

When someone remarked to them, "My, you are such good children," they gave a classic answer: "We have to be, or Grandma will put us in a book."

1

Wrightsville Beach

IN THE EARLY MORNING HOURS of May 1978, I leaned into the wind and walked the isolated, ivory-colored beach, just outside Wilmington, North Carolina, alone. Waves rushed the shoreline and washed over my sandy feet while salt spray brushed my tear-stained face. Doubt rolled over my heart. Could Harold be wrong? If not, why was I so uncertain?

Aimlessly, I marked my footprints and occasionally stooped to trace a picture or a loved one's name in the sand. I watched blindly as the waves rolled in and erased my marks — would they be erased as easily from the canvas of time?

Slowly, with the wind still in my face, I moved toward Shell Island where the children and I gathered seashells a long time ago. By this day, though, condominiums had risen from the man-made sand dunes and the sea grasses.

To reach yesterday's island, with its sun-kissed shells, we had to wade through the inlet during low tide. One day a grandfather and his young grandson forgot the hour as they walked the beach, hand in hand, and the incoming tide with its relentless undercurrent swept them out to sea. I shaded my eyes to watch the crying seagulls swoop the sky, and I longed to cry with them. They had no roots, no permanent place to call their own — and I was about to be torn from mine.

For many years we had come as a family to enjoy this beautiful seashore in the summer, but we always returned home, home to Hamilton Lakes, a suburb of Greensboro, home to our own house at 103 Bethel Spring Dale. As I walked the beach that morning, I was remembering what my husband Harold had said some months earlier. "Margaret, I believe it is God's will that we move to Wilmington."

That is what Harold had said. Just like that!

His words were as unsettling as the sea. I was accustomed to leaving our summer refuge at Wrightsville Beach and going home to Greensboro — not to Wilmington.

I wasn't too sure if it was God's will or the Danish blood of sea captains rising to draw this viking back to sea.

"That's not all, Margaret," Harold had added, defending his plan. "I believe it would be a good thing for Ralph to go too, and begin his business in that historic city."

Now my husband was using my son's career and my love of history to convince me.

I scooped up a sand crab in my hand and tried to become its friend. As I watched, it squirmed to be free so

I dropped it into the wet sand, and my "friend" scurried away and into a safe place, hidden from the world.

Now I was squirming, not wanting to be scooped up out of my safe place—my home—and away from our neighbors, friends, family and work. I wanted to enjoy the beach for summertime—not all the time—and then crawl back into my own safe place. I didn't want to move away from our Greensboro house on the knoll, that overlooked beautiful Hamilton Lake.

While the wheels of "progress" were in motion, I stood still.

I was one of the "creatures here below"
who joined a seagull to praise Him—
even when I was still squirming.

Harold and our son, Ralph, viewed out the promised land in Wilmington, looked over the housing situation, and explored business opportunities.

Chris, Ralph's wife, waited with their two young sons, Shawn and Eric, and planned for baby Sarah's arrival. Chris gathered her little ones and rocked and prayed. She, too, desired to be snug in her safe place rather than to "squirm" in the land of the unknown.

While the men enthusiastically marched into new challenges, Chris and I prayed and shed our silent tears.

Then it was settled!

Two houses about ten minutes from the beach, a block apart, had been found in Wilmington; one of them had a shop at the rear that Ralph could use for his business. *The Master's Touch*, the reproduction and restoration of 18th century furniture, had found a home.

We had all prayed together asking God's guidance, and as the men viewed the promised land and returned with the answers to prayer, we knew it was right and in order. But my heart wouldn't move.

So today I walked the Wrightsville Beach. "Oh, Lord, I'm too old to make such drastic changes. Besides," I reminded Him, "I just planted new grass and flowers, and we just redecorated our home. And that's not all, Lord; I really don't trust all these 'wonderful' ideas!"

The seagulls kept crying. The wind still blew in my face and the waves still washed over my sandy feet. After a while, as I trudged alone on the deserted beach, a soft quietness rolled in with the rhythmic sound of the ocean waves. The seagulls soared higher and higher, and finally flew out to meet the shrimp boats. Across the breeze came a gentle whisper into my heart, "Trust Me, Margaret — just trust Me."

Rising up within me came the familiar words:

Trust in the LORD with all thine heart; and lean not unto thine own understanding. In all thy ways acknowledge him, and he shall direct thy paths (Proverbs 3:5,6).

The cloud of doubt drifted and quietly blended into the summer breeze of hope. I sensed that out of the *all things* God speaks of, He was at work for good. Yet deep inside I held a fear of change. God knew that. He knew my heart. God's love is patient and full of understanding. He even waits for us.

"What do I do next?" I called out to the sea.

A lone seagull returned and flew close to my head and I know I heard, "Praise Him! Praise Him!" Then the bird flew away, his wings lifting him out of sight.

I did! I praised my Lord.

Softly, I sang with my face to the sky, "Praise God, from whom all blessings flow." I was one of the "creatures here below" who joined a seagull to praise Him — even when I was still squirming.

Out there on the beach, the sound of the ocean was like a gentle roll of drums, urging faith to step into the water and start the believing before the seeing.

That was when the battle began — the conflict between good and best, doubt and faith — and that was when I began to struggle with a dream that wouldn't let go.

2

The Uprooted Dream

ON MY FORTIETH BIRTHDAY I had written a letter to myself, a letter filled with dreams for the next forty years. I was counting on going beyond the biblical three score and ten. The letter was to be opened on my 50th birthday, then on my 60th—just to mark off the dreams that came true.

Now I am 74 and the letter is still with me—but the dreams? That is another story! Most of them rolled out with the tide, washed away like sand castles on the shore.

My childhood memories of the Canadian prairie had placed a dream of a farm deep inside me. In my letter, I drew up plans for the farm: for cows and chickens, gardens and flowers, shade trees and swings, verandas and rocking chairs.

The letter was filled with the laughter of children and grandchildren, along with the song of birds, and barking dogs and meowing kittens and wobbly legged calves. Through the words I saw a movie in living color, with green pastures and grazing brown horses, and children riding bronze ponies. Throughout the years I had filled wastebaskets with my poems about *my dream farm.*

Then crashing into my dream came the nightmare of war in Vietnam!

By this time, Janice Dawn, our first-born, was happily married to Judson Carlberg. Our younger son, Ralph, was in school. Harold traveled throughout many of the eastern and southern states, and I was the infirmary nurse at Greensboro College.

With tears in our hearts, Harold and I had watched our lanky, blue-eyed Dan, our elder son, board a train in Raleigh—destination: Vietnam.

"Don't worry about me, Mom," he had told me. "I have the armor of God over my army uniform. I'll be home again!"

With a chug of its engine, and a clang of its wheels, the train pulled away. It was Sunday morning and we found ourselves driving teary-eyed toward church. During the communion service someone sang, "Fill my cup, Lord. I lift it up, Lord . . ."

I felt drained and empty; doubt fought to remove the faith I struggled to keep. Yet soon God's peace quietly filled my cup and His love enveloped me in His presence. I was in a safe place.

While letters and packages flew across the miles, I marked the days on a calendar. Each month I embroidered a square for a quilt, marking Dan's year in Vietnam; each square had a message of hope. My journal began to fill up with God's promises.

> All thy children shall be taught of the LORD; and great shall be the peace of thy children (Isaiah 54:13).

> I will contend with him that contendeth with thee, and I will save thy children (Isaiah 49:25).

Lena Rogers Leach,[1] the beloved maid who worked with me in the infirmary at Greensboro College, joined me in the battle to believe. Lena, with her shiny ebony skin and wide, dark eyes, had fought more than one spiritual battle for the college students at Greensboro. Now her heart of love included my sons.

My dream of a farm was held suspended between these two wars.

The battle was fought not only for Dan in Vietnam, but also for Ralph. He was held hostage by the enemy in a war zone of rebellion against God's authority—location: New England.

Dan's war was fought with guns and tanks; the war for Ralph, a spiritual war, was not fought with conventional weapons but with the sword of the Word of God and the shield of faith.

My dream of a farm was held suspended between these two wars.

Then in November 1969, Dan came home. For Dan, the war was over. He came home with a dream—like mine—a dream of a farm where all the family could come, for reunions, or even to live. While Dan taught school in the mountains, he drew up plans.

"Just listen to that child talk!" Lena threw back her head and laughed joyously as she listened to Dan spill out his dream.

" 'Families should not be separated.' That's what our child says. 'God never intended folks to be torn apart.' Lord, have mercy! Dan thinks Lena is coming to that farm to cook corn bread and fry chicken for all the Jensens coming down the road!"

Lena and I plastered pictures of farms all over the kitchen walls of the college infirmary. "We have the farm in our heads. Now all we need is some land to put it on," I sighed.

Laughter filled the infirmary kitchen, and hope flooded our hearts.

Lena folded her arms across her ample bosom. "That's not all—our child Ralph is coming home. God done told us that. Now we just wait to see how God works His plan out. We just trust and obey." And she went back to the tiny kitchen to heat some "Lena tea," humming while she worked.

One day Lena picked up the newspaper on her way to the college. Over a cup of coffee, we began our Bible study and prayer. Then Lena opened the paper.

"Look at this, Nurse Jensen. This could be Dan's land—66 acres near Stoneville—that little town thirty miles from here. Just wait till Dan comes from school and we show him this paper."

Lena got a beat—then hummed a tune; soon the words came:

> Go out there, Dan,
> Possess the land.
> We move one step at the time.

We walk by faith,
Not by sight.
We move one step at the time.
The Word's a lamp;
The Word's a light.
We move one step at the time.
We walk by faith;
Not by sight.
We move one step at the time.

We had our theme song!

Once again I read the letter I wrote myself on my 40th birthday. Twenty years had passed and at long last it seemed my dreams were coming true.

Then Ralph came home! Our tall, lean son—our handsome, southern blue-eyed boy—had gone off to a Christian college with the seeds of rebellion already stirring inside him. We almost lost him to the quicksands of sin. He came back as a stranger—gaunt, bearded, long-haired, hunched over in his fleece-lined jacket. Then in the midst of the rebellion, God worked His miracle in Ralph's life, turning him around and really bringing him home—home to God; home to us. The war had been won and heaven and earth rang with "Amazing grace! How sweet the sound!"

Out on Dan's farm near Stoneville, which now was expanding to include a place for the boys' hippie friends to come for food and lodging, with machete in hand, Ralph carved a path through the brush to the gurgling spring. Dan bulldozed the scrub fields and made a pasture for

Ginger, the horse, and perhaps the wobbly legged calves I saw in my dream. Together we planted fruit trees and gardens while the valley rang with the sound of saws and hammers.

The log cabin at our farm was replaced with a chalet-type lodge house, which Harold and Dan designed and built. It had cedar siding and open beams. A wide stairway brought us to the second and third floors where the view stretched to hazy blue mountains and Hanging· Rock, a favorite scenic ridge. It would be a place where hippies were welcome to come for food and lodging.

One by one, Ralph's old friends came to see what had happened to Ralph and if, indeed, he was a new creation. They saw the valley and stayed; later, they saw the miracle of God's love.

Guitars strummed into the night accompanied by whippoorwills calling to each other while stars watched.

"Families shouldn't be separated," Dan had said.

Lena nodded. "Too much hurt in the world. Folks need each other, and a place to come to—a time for healing from this hurting world. Why, Dan child, you be like Moses fixing to bring us all into the Promised Land."

Lena's laughter rang out while we watched the lodge develop and the land overgrown with scrub trees and weeds bloom into a beautiful valley of flowers and gardens. The freezers were filled.

After Harold helped Dan acquire the 66 acres, Harold and I purchased the adjoining 38 acres. Across the valley, Doris and David Hammer, my sister and her husband, built their beautiful colonial home overlooking the valley. Across their road stood the yellow house built for our Norwegian mama and papa.

But Mama came alone. Papa never saw the desk and books in his new study. God took him home to meet the Author of his faith — and the authors of his treasured books.

Once again I read the letter I wrote myself on my 40th birthday. Twenty years had passed and at long last it seemed my dreams were coming true.

Dan marked off building sites. Jan and Jud would have a place to build a house or a cabin for summer vacations, and even for their retirement in years to come. There would be room for relatives on plots of ground in our combined acreage.

My dreams soared. All my life I had moved from place to place, never close to anyone I could call my own. As a child I envied my friends with relatives so I called older friends "aunt" or "uncle."

Now Uncle Howard, Uncle Jack, and the sisters could all come. No one would ever be lonely again.

Doris and Dave had 150 acres. Combined, Dan and Harold and I had more than a hundred acres. My brother Gordon from New York bought adjoining property.

For five years our family poured strength, creativity and money into our dream. Dan's chalet neared completion and our house was sited on a knoll. No one would be separated again.

"We all need a place to come home to," Willie from the children's home had told Mama.

I was confident that love would cover the valley with a blanket of peace.

Late into the night, we sat around the dining room table in the house on Bethel Spring Dale in Greensboro and ideas flowed on paper as well as through excited conversation.

We called Highway 220 North the Glory Road while our cars brought food, supplies and people to our Promised Land. One guest, an artist, watched the valley below from the third floor of the lodge. "I'll just bring my canvas and paint and put all this in permanent color," he said.

"That's not all. I'll come up here and write books about all that's going on," I answered. "You paint the dream with oil, and I'll paint it with words."

We laughed together. The blending of a dream makes a joyful sound.

"Missionaries on furlough should have their own home, a place where they can spend time with their families and where they can share in Bible study and prayer with other families," I suggested.

"We need recreational facilities—tennis courts, and a swimming pool," Ralph insisted. "Even a lake, stocked with fish."

The ideas flowed like mountain streams, fresh and challenging. Dan named the place Shalom Valley Farm, the place of peace and wholeness. Shalom Valley was carved in wood and etched in our hearts.

And then, suddenly, before the chalet was completed, the dream was gone!

Our sky turned black for us. Thunder rolled, and in fury a cold wind swept darkening clouds across the valley. The trees bent in sorrow and the valley seemed to weep while the uprooted dreams perished in the storm of life.

Today the unfinished lodge, still empty, stands alone on its 66 acres, "for sale." The wind slaps against the windows, seeking an entrance. The fruit trees we planted are withered and the fruit on the vines has died. The wild grasses grow again over the valley and the lonely cry of the whippoorwill calls into the night. Standing guard over the lonely house, towering pines reach to the skies as the valley sobs out its sorrow. The dreams are dead, and the song is not sung.

"Where are you, Lord?" I cried over the valley in the day of destruction. "No! No! My dream can't die! The music can't die now! For fifty years I've held this dream in my heart—no, no, not now, not when it finally seems to be coming true. Now it is gone!"

We wiped our tears and left the house—so alone—in the setting of God's surrounding beauty.

My anguish was unbearable. "We prayed, believed, walked and worked together step by step—and, Lord, it was such a good dream. It really was—and a blessing to so many people. Why, Lord?"

Sometimes God answers in silence. This was one of those times—God was silent!

And so it came to pass that Dan went away. He took his beautiful bride to follow another dream—somewhere in the West—where they would build their own little nest. And our dream of a farm for the family was uprooted.

And then it also came to pass that Harold said, "Come, Margaret. I believe it is God's will that we move to Wilmington."

And Ralph said, "Come, Chris, for when God closes one door, He opens another."

He did!

Many months later, after the sharp pain had faded somewhat and turned to a dull ache that never goes away, Harold and I returned to Shalom. On a hazy fall day we walked hand in hand down the overgrown path to stand beside the foundation Ralph had begun for his home. The furniture shop was to have been down by the spring.

We looked at the knoll where we had marked off our house. My sister Doris and I had laughed about each having a flagpole so we could hoist a signal when the coffee pot was on.

We had said, "When our house sells in Greensboro, then we'll begin to build on Shalom." We wondered why our house didn't sell then — but God knew. God had a plan. Later, long after the weeds had grown back at the farm, when Harold said we should go to Wilmington, the first person who looked at our Greensboro home bought it. God's timing!

The valley was gold and red. A quiet peace covered the land. Harold and I wept as we stood beside the empty lodge that Harold had helped to build. Three years of his hard work. We could hear again the hammers and saws, the laughter, and the songs from our "hippy boys." We loved them "as is" — God changed them "as His."

Doris and Dave's colonial house still stands high on the hill overlooking the silent valley of Shalom. My brother Gordon died before he could come to his place. And the wind blows through Dan's unfinished lodge.

I remembered a verse I had written in my journal when I first saw the land:

> *A land which the LORD thy God careth for: the eyes of the LORD thy God are always upon it, from the beginning of the year even unto the end of the year (Deuteronomy 11:12).*

We turned to look again at the valley with its patchwork quilt of gold, yellow and red. The towering pines swept the sky—strong, green and unbending. When we closed the gate, we wiped our tears and left the lodge—so alone—in the setting of God's surrounding beauty. "Keep your eye on it, Lord; please keep your eye on it."

A dream was marked, *For Sale!*

We didn't go back again!

1. Editors note: You can read about Lena in Margaret Jensen's book, *Lena*, published by Here's Life Publishers, San Bernardino, CA, © 1985.

"I Want My Own Crib!"

"BUT, GRAMMY, I don't want a new bed. I want my own crib." Three-year-old Eric was sobbing his heart out.

"But, Eric, you are a big boy now and Sarah needs your crib."

"She can have another crib. I want my own crib — and I don't want to be a big boy." The tears kept coming.

While Ralph's wife Chris was tending the new baby in Greensboro, we had gone ahead to Wilmington with their two boys, Shawn and Eric, to get the furniture in place. Harold already had spent several days painting each room as a special surprise for Chris.

When the moving van left, Chris said to us, "Just pile the boxes in the living room. I'll get to it later."

Wistfully she had watched us leave, then rocked Sarah, her new baby girl, and prayed. She, too, had learned to "trust in the LORD with all your heart."

When I arrived on the scene in Wilmington, my Norwegian heritage marched to the call of duty, and scrub brush and soap found the corners.

Baby Sarah's room was painted yellow and white, and Eric's crib was settled into one corner. The chest of drawers also had been painted yellow and white and matching curtains framed the newly washed windows. Our Norwegian Bestemor's rocking chair sat in another corner waiting for Chris and Sarah.

The next day, Chris and Sarah arrived and we all greeted them with a shout of welcome. My sister Grace had brought them from Greensboro to their new home. Ralph escorted them over the threshold.

Curled up in my arm, Eric fell asleep, blanket and teddy bear held close.

"But I want my own crib," Eric wailed.

"We'll have lunch first and then we'll talk about the crib," I told him. "Just look at that beautiful baby — like a little doll."

Eric agreed and finally smiled.

I poured the coffee and looked for Chris. I found her sitting in Bestemor's rocker — with tears on her cheeks. I understood! She had found a safe place, and for a few moments she had to squirm out of the hand of the unknown and wriggle into that safe place.

She was home!

Brick by brick, and promise upon promise from God's Word, she would build her house, and the storms of life would not blow the house down.

"Come, Eric," I said, "you and I will take a nap on your new bed. You hold your teddy bear and I'll hold you. Shawn will take his blanket and sleep on his new bed."

Curled up in my arm, Eric fell asleep, blanket and teddy bear held close. Shawn held his blanket and fell fast asleep too. And God held us close to Himself—teddy bear, blankets and all.

> Bless this house, Oh, Lord.
> Keep it safe.
> Let Your eye be upon it
> From the beginning of the year
> Even to the end of it.

When our refreshing nap was over, Eric crawled up in my lap. "I like my new bed and I'm a big boy now," he confided. "Sarah can have my crib." He too, had found a safe place.

But I was still squirming. I wanted my own dream.

4

The Troll

OUR NORWEGIAN PAPA had passed his favorite stories on to his children. In turn, each generation passes them on, and each new generation gets a revised version of an old text.

One legend is about an old farmer in Norway who was tormented by a troll. Now, in Scandinavian folklore, a troll can be a giant or a mischievous dwarf—but a troll always spells trouble!

Sometimes the old farmer's cow would refuse to give milk, the hens would stop laying eggs, and the gardens wouldn't produce. Only a troll could cause such disasters.

One day the farmer decided to take his family and his belongings in the old wagon and sneak quietly away in the dark of night. He would leave that troll behind forever!

The wagon moved slowly down the road and the farmer chuckled to himself. "Ja, now we will be free from that old troll at last."

The farmer's wife happily agreed. Their troubles were over!

Suddenly, from under the wagon, up jumped the troll with, "Moving, are we?"

Now, Ralph and I were moving!

Harold and Chris were in Wilmington, and Ralph and I had returned to gather up the odds and ends in Greensboro.

Plants filled the back seat of our weather-beaten car; yucca bushes were sticking out of the windows—even prickly leaves escaped from the trunk.

And our troll was with us!

Vicky, our black labrador retriever, was curled up at my feet by the front seat.

From behind the wheel, Ralph verbalized my feelings when he said, "Well, Mom, we're leaving it all behind; we'll soon be on our way. I'm not sure if we should laugh or cry."

That choice was made for us. When Ralph started the car, our "giant troll" jumped up into my lap like a frightened kitten and refused to move. There she sat, all 100 pounds of her, looking out the window. Together we were framed in yucca bushes.

At the traffic light a trucker leaned out of his cab and burst into laughter. "Now, I've seen everything!" he called.

"The Beverly Hillbillies've got nothin' on us," I yelled back.

Between the prickly leaves and our "troll" with her hot breath in our faces, there was no time for tears.

---

*Harold stared at us with his mouth open.
"I can't believe you!"*

When we pulled into our driveway in Wilmington five long hours later, Harold stared at us with his mouth open. "I can't believe you!" He wasn't laughing.

Harold unloaded all the plants and prickly bushes. I limped around to get circulation back into my legs. Vicky, the troll, was off looking for holes to dig and squirrels to chase. And Ralph drove on to his home a block away.

When we viewed the challenge before us, Harold's "Moving, are we?" — taken directly from the troll story — brought the laughter. This was no time for tears, either.

I walked through the freshly painted rooms where love had prepared a way for dragging feet and a doubting heart. A new stove stood in the kitchen and I knew that signaled #1 priority. When I saw the bedroom in order — that was #2 priority.

It was the screened-in porch that challenged us. Furniture and boxes were piled high out there and somehow it seemed to me that my life consisted of boxes to be emptied. "I think that 'troll' from Norway keeps them filled," I told Harold.

I remembered the long ago time when as a fourteen-year-old I told Mama, "The world is so mixed up, Mama, I could die."

"Oh, Ja, so while you are dying — iron!"

Mama pulled the clothes basket from under the kitchen table — and I ironed! When suppertime came I sat down to meatballs and mashed potatoes. I had forgotten about dying.

I now viewed seven rooms of furniture to be placed into five small rooms, but decided, like Scarlet in *Gone With the Wind,* "I'll think about that tomorrow."

I heard again, "Ja, when you are dying — iron!" So I did!

With that shiny new stove looking at me, I decided to prepare a special meal. Tomorrow was another day. Tonight we would enjoy a steak and mashed potatoes, and be thankful that Ralph, Chris and the children were only a block away.

The next day Ralph put a $2 ad in the paper, and, closing the door to security, he walked through the gateway into a challenging future. Turning his face to the wind, he fixed his heart on God and planted his feet on the firm foundation — God's promises.

The storms would come, the winds would blow, but his house of faith would stand. It was built on the Rock.

"A man has to have a dream — he can't live without a dream," he told us. "God gave me a dream — *The Master's Touch.*" The dream began with restoration of two chairs. It lives on in homes enriched with Ralph's 18th-century reproductions. The lessons of faith continue for a lifetime.

A Georgian table, hand carved with a pocket knife, graces our living room today — a reminder of the Master's Touch on hearts of stone or pieces of wood. God's creative touch has no limits.

5

Bloom Where You Are Planted

THE NEXT MORNING, I watched the hanging fern in the early morning sun. A gentle breeze blew across my face and a whisper of hope slipped into my heart.

"Bloom where you are planted, Mother." Jan, our daughter in Massachusetts, sent cards and notes almost daily to remind me of God's promises and His faithfulness in all circumstances of life. Even a move.

The plant from Jan was a daily reminder for me — to bloom!

Harold and I arranged our wall-to-wall furniture and our too many pictures. Bookcases made room dividers and the dining room invaded the living room. For the first time, I had no formal dining room, and when family and guests squeezed around the table no one could get out. Eric usually managed to crawl under the table with the magic whisper, "Bathroom, Grammy."

The kitchen and bedrooms had the priority of Norwegian order. Plastic buckets became the emergency second bathroom. The house was small, but the weed-filled yard made it all like an overgrown, abandoned farm. I stood in the doorway, hands on hips, staring gloomily outside.

"Guess we'll have to do what we can with what we have!" I said.

After forty years, it seemed we were starting all over again. So we went forth like conquering generals, armed with rakes, shovels and hoes. The yucca bushes, forty-five in number, made a prickly fence by College Road bordering the side of our large lot. The university was just across that road.

I suspected that all those encouraging notes and cards had helped to keep her own faith going.

We planted everything we could get at a bargain. The desert began to bloom like a rose. Harold splurged and bought ten palm trees. Pampas grass, holly bushes and azaleas filled empty spaces. In the spring I would get a bed for my zinnias and we'd plant a vegetable garden.

Jan and her husband, Jud, were coming with their little ones, Heather and Chad. The guest room was ready and the children would share a hide-a-bed. (When they grew older we'd put cots in the living room).

The car pulled up and with squeals of laughter the children ran through the expanse of gardens.

"Oh, Mother, I dreaded to come to a new place and I knew I would miss my old room and the children would miss Gramma's attic."

(I suspected that all those encouraging notes and cards, even the hanging basket, had helped to keep her own faith going.)

"And the pool—I was sure everyone would miss the pool, but we have the ocean! Look, Jud, even woods all across the back! It's like a mini farm."

(I must not think about the farm and the lonely house.)

Chris had made a wall plaque:

```
Small Houses
Filled With Love
Have Elastic Walls.
```

"Mother, Dad, it is home!" Jan exclaimed. "This is home! It's like it has always been—and I don't even miss the Bethel Spring Dale house."

I didn't tell her how I had driven back to Greensboro and sat by Lake Hamilton, looking up at my house on the knoll, crying because of the strangers in it. I cried then. I'm not crying anymore. I squared my shoulders. "Let's all walk out on the pier after supper; we can swim tomorrow."

After their favorite meal of meatballs, mashed potatoes and cherry pie, we walked on the pier, and we watched a fisherman, and we sat on the benches with our feet up on the rail and listened to the roll of the ocean and the slap of waves against the pilings.

"We've come here before—many summers," we told the children. "We used to rent a place on Crane Drive by the ocean and I loved to read in a hammock on the veranda. We didn't have air conditioning, but the ocean breeze blew through the house and we didn't care if the sheets were damp and sandy."

Heather and Chad leaned against me, and I went on. "I can remember when your grandpa and I would slip out of bed early in the morning to take a quiet walk on the beach while your mother and her brothers were still asleep. Your mother would always hear us and wake the boys. Your grandfather would say, 'Don't look now, Margaret, but I think three musketeers are following us.' When we peeked around we would see two sleepy boys in their pajamas following their adored sister."

I looked at my grandchildren. "When the summer was over your mother and uncles looked like brown Indians. I'm sure you will look like that, too, when you go home."

"Time for ice cream!" We jumped to our feet and Harold marched us all to the ice cream parlor. Some traditions never die.

The day came to a close and everyone was tucked into bed.

"If you should awaken in the night, Heather, and have leg aches (egg lakes, she called them) or a bad dream—after your long ride in the car—just come into our bed. Don't disturb your parents. They are weary after driving so far."

The house grew still. Everyone was asleep.

When morning came, Heather was asleep in my arm. Chad was curled up in his Papa's arm. The had found their safe place in our new home in Wilmington.

He hideth my soul in the cleft of the Rock . . .
And covers me there with His Hand.

6

The House of Joy

I HATED TO ADMIT IT, but life in Wilmington was marvelous. It was just like old times. Our little house was bursting with company. My sisters, Doris and Grace, were there. Cots were already made up for them in the den and the living room.

And Lena was there! Lena, who saw the changing times with me but knew the God who never changes, had come for a visit, and when she arrived we laughed and hugged so much we couldn't talk.

Harold grinned at me, his eyes twinkling as if to say, *You womenfolk need to be left alone so you can catch up on your do-you-remembers.* Then he picked up her suitcase. "I'll put this in the guest room for you, Lena."

I kept smiling at my friend as she bounced around our living room. Her ebony skin glowed and her deep brown eyes took in everything. She hurried through the house, with Doris, Grace and me at her heels, and we all enjoyed the inspection tour.

She paused at the family photographs in the hall and bedroom and gently outlined the faces of Dan and Ralph. She had loved those boys and prayed for them so often when we worked together at the college infirmary.

"I've been calling your name," she said as she touched Ralph's picture. Then she turned to me. "Lands, Margaret, look at all of this. Lord have mercy, child! I hope you asked the Lord to forgive you for all the tears you shed when you had to move from that Bethel place." She shook her head, but her expression was loving. "How is it that you forgot all those tears for the family, tears for those hippy boys—and all the weeping for your sons? No wonder Lake Hamilton is running over. You put enough tears in it—watered the woods, too."

Lena marched around the house again. "Oh, glory, this house is a house of joy. Margaret, you put that farm and Bethel Place to rest, and you start praising God for a house of joy."

Back in the kitchen, I put the coffeepot on—the only thing to do when my sisters and Lena come. As we sat around the table, Lena sipped her coffee from the china cup, and then set it down.

"Margaret, you got some instant coffee? This coffee too weak for Lena."

My sisters agreed! So I made it stronger and we laughed and talked together while we munched oven-fresh cinnamon rolls and drank the stronger coffee.

"What we really need," I told my sisters, "is some of Lena's tea and her pound cake. She's the queen of pound cakes."

Lena beamed. "Go on with you. Just nothing wrong with these cinnamon rolls of yours."

An hour later, we changed into our bathing suits — Lena with much urging — and headed for the beach. She toed the water gingerly, then plunged ahead, braving the waves with the delight of a child. She beckoned my sisters to follow, and soon we were all jumping the waves. When the waves would knock Lena down, her laughter was contagious.

After one of them, she said, "Just like life! Some waves plumb knock you over, but then you get up and keep going until another wave hits you."

"I kept telling your Grandma,
'The believing come before the seeing.'"

She was down again and we laughed together, almost losing our footing as we helped her up.

"We are in a battle, children. No way we get rest on this earth — no, not 'til Jesus comes. Praise God. When the battle's over, we shall wear a crown — but the battle's not over yet."

Another wave and we all went down!

"Look at the storm we've been through — and re-member, children, the best part is we go *through* the storm; we don't stay in it."

We got out of the waves. Enough is enough!

With towels wrapped around us we sang all the way home.

"Nothing like a warm shower and clean clothes — a blessing, children, a great blessing. Oh, God is so good to His children — all the little things every day that comes our way. Blessings — that's what they are — blessings."

We joined Ralph and his family at Balentine's Cafeteria later, and Ralph crushed Lena against him with a bear hug. The children were excited to be with Lena.

"This my child," Lena announced to the children. "Yes, sir, this my child."

Ralph still had his arm around Lena.

"I birthed him in the spirit. Took some powerful praying and believing, but he came home. Oh, glory to Jesus, he came home. I kept telling your Grandma — 'The believing come before the seeing.'"

I didn't know whether to laugh or cry remembering those times of praying in the infirmary. "Lena used to march me around singing," I told the children, "praying for your daddy."

Lena nodded. "We could have us a shouting time right here in the cafeteria."

I glanced hastily at Harold. I was getting worried — she might just do that.

"Here we are — all of us together. God did that. God's grace. His love makes us all one and the past is gone and we walk the rest of the way by faith."

The children warmed to Lena, and she to them. She'd pause between bites of dinner just smiling at them and then at their daddy. "I'll be calling out your names," she told them.

I knew that when she was in bed that night she would cry out, "This is Lena, Lord. I want to talk to you about Eric and Shawn, Sarah and Kathryn. Them's Ralph's children. I want to be thanking you for them."

When we returned home, we had us a "praising time," a time filled with laughter, rejoicing, and thanksgiving for the mercies of God.

Lena sang her theme song:

> Without Him I would be nothing . . .
> Like a ship without a sail.

" 'I know My plans for you — and My plans are good.' That's God talking, Margaret."

Together we recalled the blessings of God — the days at Greensboro College, the time Lena met Mr. Leach, and the days since then. Soon after she met that gentle elderly widower, she came in and held up the engagement ring he had given her and announced their wedding plans. After a quiet wedding we had a happy celebration in our home. Since then they have served the Lord together.

Mr. Leach tends his garden, smiles and shakes his head at Lena's persistent witness. His witness is a quiet, steady Christian walk. They make a good pair. Lena turned Mr. Leach's lonely house into a house of joy where many come to pray and leave with burdens lifted.

Having Lena with us stirred other memories. I looked around at our happy circle — Harold, my dear sisters, my son and grandchildren and Lena, and thought of the years that had passed.

The infirmary days were ended, and Lena obtained other parttime work—always serving the Lord with joy.

Doris and Dave keep watch over the valley, and their beautiful home draws the family together often. We like to gather there for reunions, and we come from all directions like moths to a flame.

Grace has continually encircled the family with prayer, and she remembers how God has led her one step at a time.

I thought about Joyce and Howard (my other sister and Harold's brother who are married to each other). Their dreams had changed and had brought them close to their family in Arkansas. My thoughts then moved to my youngest sister, Jeanelle, and how she watched a dream die with the song not sung, but how, through it all, her faith in God emerged in strength and power. Her children call her blessed.

I told Lena again how when Papa went home in 1973, Mama moved into the yellow house—alone, yet not alone. "I am with you always."

She nodded as I added, "Gordon, our only brother, joined our father in 1975. His widow Alice walks with God—she knows that He promised never to leave her or forsake her. Their dreams also died—the song not sung." I had to stop and take a deep breath before I could go on to say, "And then, just two years ago, in 1977, Mama went home and joined the others."

"You never mind, child," Lena said softly. "We all have our dreams, but through the tapestry of dark and golden threads God weaves His plan. You just be thinkin', 'I know My plans for you—and My plans are good.' That's God talking, Margaret, and no good thing will He withhold from us who love Him."

Her foot was already tapping out the music, a song of heaven. We sang the songs of faith together, confident that God would complete what He had begun in our lives—even if the plans we made fell apart. His ways are higher—and someday we would see clearly.

The day came to a close, and the house of joy grew quiet, while the warm breezes blew softly through the pampas grass. Slowly, steadily, the house of joy became also a house of peace and rest.

A new day, with stronger coffee, brought us all to life again. Too soon the visit came to an end and the car pulled out of the driveway, taking Lena with it.

I turned back to the duties of the day, but I paused for a moment—smiling at the Lord, smiling at the memory of Lena's visit.

"I'm giving thanks, Lena," I said, "It's a blessing— work and a house of joy."

7

The Changing Winds

A COOL MIST brushed my face one morning in 1981. I wrapped my jacket around me and fastened my headscarf tighter. My tennis shoes made a pattern in the moist sand.

When I threw bread crusts into the air, the seagulls made a game of catching the bread mid-air and flying off with it to an accompanying angry chorus of their envious brothers.

Tourists had gathered their chairs, umbrellas and ice chests, had closed their summer houses, and had made their way back to work and school, and the beach was deserted. The wind sighed with relief.

We enjoyed each other, the seagulls and I, until the bread ran out and they headed out to sea. "Desert me, then," I called after them. I was left alone with the roll of the ocean and the wind in the seagrass.

An old song came to mind as I walked the beach:

> Wonderful grace of Jesus,
> greater than the mighty rolling sea.

I rounded a large sand dune and a colorful seashell caught my eye. Its delicate design reminded me of how fearfully and wonderfully we all are made.

"I had a dream — but God has a plan" kept returning to me from my journal notes.

As far as the eye could see, the waves rolled in.

> I watched the churning waves
> With splashing foam and fury
> Stop — then,
> Gently touch the sand,
> Held by His Hand,
> Held by His Hand.

In my Bible I had written:

> *It is in the process, not with the end result, where we learn to praise and give thanks. We don't need to see the shore or the waves. We just need to see Jesus.*

It was a long ago time when I first had walked the beach and wondered at the will of God. *Trust me* came the answer. Now the days, months and years had stretched into a walk of faith. Even so, the pain of the shattered dreams had become a dull ache, an ever-present silent companion who stayed hidden under the endless tasks occupying my hands. My thoughts kept going back.

The house of joy was small, but with the elastic walls of love, it had replaced the house on the knoll. My "dream house" had become a gentle memory. Even the tears were almost forgotten.

While I walked the beach, I pondered how such good dreams could take such an upside-down turn. Yet deep in my heart I knew that out of what sometimes seems all wrong to us, God often brings untold blessings. Even if our desires conflict with God's perfect will, it is not the end of the world—God still can take the "all things" and work them for good. Sometimes we run ahead and miss God's caution lights. Yet we can always come back to the cross and examine our motives, and then we see His hand in it all.

Now, 20 years later, we see how God allowed our detours. He was there all the time. He never forsakes His own. There are some things we will never understand, but we know Him, and His promises never fail. "Trust and obey—there is no other way."

The sounds of a coming storm blew across the sea grasses and the sand swirled in my face. It was time to leave my trysting place.

On March 17, 1981, the blue house a block away from us was bursting with life. Kathryn Elise had arrived on the scene. Later, when she grew older, she informed the world, "I was born on St Patrick's Day and I don't even like green. Besides, I'm Norwegian and I like potatoes."

From the day she was born, her brother Eric adored her, and he immediately took charge of the new baby. Today they not only share a special love for each other, but they also share a capacity for mischief. Sarah and Shawn pursue projects; Eric and Kathryn pursue pleasure.

Ralph's small shop on the rear of his lot began to stretch and groan until *The Master's Touch* had to move into a new home on Myrtle Grove Road, five miles closer to the sound. While Ralph kept busy at his furniture store, the tricycles and bikes made a path to my door; the kids came for cookies — Chris for coffee. I kept the coffee hot and the cookie jar filled as we laughed and cried together.

When my daughter Jan and her family came for a visit, we all went into high gear to bring out the cots and plastic "potties" — just in case. Chris is the sister Jan would have chosen, the second daughter I would have selected. We know God brought her to us — He had a plan. We have our dreams.

Dreams! How often I found my way to the sea — just to walk the endless stretch of sand and to ponder how God holds the oceans in His hand, numbers the grains of sand and even the hairs of my head. There by the sea, I reminded God of my dreams and He, loving me, reminded me of His plans. The ocean keeps talking of the power, the grace, the mercy, and the love of God.

It was late in the morning by now, and I sat down on a log — a piece of shapeless driftwood washed to the shore. Where had it come from? Was this lumber a part of some great ship lost at sea in a storm? And I thought of Papa bringing home the lost.

"Ja, ja, I know, I know," he would say. "I keep bringing home human driftwood — so, who knows what God can do with the driftwood?"

My Norwegian papa never tired of "bringing them in," and Mama always put on the coffeepot. Now Mama and Papa are safely home in God's harbor; yet, the "driftwood" from Mama's kitchen still rises up across the land to call both Mama and Papa blessed. They did what was in their hand, and they dreamed their dreams, and they thanked God in the process. Mama didn't crumble when some of her dreams failed.

The winds of change come. It is then we learn to set our sails to catch the wind and move ahead, or we spend a lifetime battling wind and wave, dreaming our dreams, and missing the plan, the process.

I walked back through puddles to get to my car, then drove home to a hot bath and a cup of tea. Tomorrow I would get up early and write.

Across the sky the clouds gathered and the waves rolled and churned with a roar. The sounds of a coming storm blew across the sea grasses and the sand swirled in my face.

It was time to leave my trysting place, the log that was on the beach because another storm had already taken its life away. The seagulls now had their safe place and the sand crabs had burrowed into their tunnels. I headed for my safe place—home. The wind and rain slapped against the house; the thunder rolled and the lightning flashed. I was almost drenched when I reached my kitchen.

With a cup of tea and a sandwich I was all set for a stormy afternoon. A good book and a nap would bring a good day to a close.

Then the phone interrupted my thoughts — and my plans. "We need a 3-11 P.M. private duty nurse," the nursing supervisor said.

Within the hour I was on my way to the hospital, a raincoat over my white uniform, my white shoes in a bag, my eyes squinting against the blinding rain — and I realized that *life is what happens while we are making other plans.*

The windshield wipers were still beating their steady rythm as I pulled into the parking lot. I waited for the deluge to subside, and my thoughts went back to the day Shawn had called me, "Come, get me, Gramma. I'm having a hard day."

I did! A hamburger at the mall turned the day into a good day. I never asked what made it bad — but suspected a quarrel with Eric.

Now the rain came in sheets!

I remembered the day when for the first time I eased my beat-up car into the parking lot of this New Hanover Hospital. How I longed for my safe place back at the Greensboro Infirmary — here I had to face a new hospital with new doctors and new nurses. The old familiar faces from Greensboro were gone. The tears fell.

"Oh, Lord, come get me," I had cried. "I'm having a hard day."

He did! He came through strangers — Marge Du-Bois and Dr. B. Williams — and through the gracious reception from the staff. He came through the patience of Nellie Sullivan during orientation. With special grace, He came to me through the private duty nurses: Diane Satterfield, the 7-3 A.M. nurse, and Mary Jane Horell, the 11-7

A.M. nurse. From them I received a post-graduate re-fresher course. The strangers became friends.

That was a long ago yesterday. The tide of those times ebbed and flowed for many months in the same way I had come and gone through these hospital doors.

Each day holds its own routine, but deep within us we stretch and grow in the discipline of the will and commitment of the heart. We set our heart before our steps. We see from the mountaintop, but we learn in the valley. Day after day I walked in the same routine that seemed to go nowhere, but the lessons of faith were being etched for a lifetime.

I glanced at my watch. The rain didn't want to stop so I made a dash for the open door. With umbrella, raincoat and boots tucked away, I took the elevator to the ninth floor to report for duty.

When 11 P.M. came, I walked back through puddles to get to my car, then drove home to a hot bath and a cup of tea. The relentless rain of the afternoon had made a nest for the lessons of faith etched in my memory, and they wouldn't let go of me. I made a decision that night. Tomorrow I would get up early and write.

So I gathered the notes I had tucked away through the years and began to put them together into written words for the family to remember. These stories would not be lost to my children and grandchildren.

And so my first book, *First We Have Coffee*[1] came into being. I had a dream—God had a plan.

---

1. Published by Here's Life Publishers, San Bernardino, CA, ©1982.

8

The Blue Datsun

"WHEN YOU DIE, GRAMMY, can I have the Blue Datsun?"

To five-year-old Kathryn, the Blue Datsun was the golden chariot that carried Cinderella to the ball, the Roman chariot in Ben Hur, or the old reliable that carried sand buckets, big towels and excited young 'uns to the beach.

"The way it looks right now, Kathryn, the Blue Datsun will die before I do, but if she lives, you certainly can have her."

Kathryn was happy. The Blue Datsun would remain in the family forever.

For some reason the Blue Datsun was a "her" — a part of the family. We talked to her, pleaded with her, screamed at her — even cried over her. We sympathized with her as she aged and became increasingly bent, broken and bruised.

The Blue Datsun hadn't always looked like that. At one time she was shining and new. One look at her and I knew I had a friend who could face the challenges of the roads of life with me.

The students at Greensboro College admired my excellent choice and she was the envy of the campus. Everything else in the parking lot paled beside her shining blue armor.

One day our elder son Dan took her into the North, and my Dixie Datsun collided with a Yankee Ford. She hadn't known the war was over, and she came limping home, wounded and depressed. Her battle scars healed eventually, though, and once again she gamely hit the road.

One Christmas Eve, Ralph and his friend Billy were crossing an icy bridge on their way home for our special Christmas Eve dinner. The brave little Datsun was hit by an oncoming car. Apparently the driver was under the influence of the deadly enemy, drugs. The Datsun smashed into the railing, but it held fast, and the boys were kept from going into the frigid river below. The occupants of the other car also were spared and Ralph and Billy shared their faith with them while waiting for the police to come. Our Christmas Eve dinner was a little late that night, but our hearts were filled with gratitude that all the lives had been spared.

The Blue Datsun proudly wore the "purple heart" awarded her for bravery and for injury in action, but the scars were beginning to show. Her rusted-out trunk held a board across the holes, and sand buckets and inner tubes (used as ocean liners) found a special place there. The plastic seats were held together with dark blue tape, and wet bathing suits, sticky fingers and gum wrappers found a happy home there.

Her air conditioning worked only in the winter so in the summer all the windows would be open and the wind would blow on the children while they sang:

> Sea gull, sea gull,
> Up in the sky —
> We can see you flying so high.
> Please, please, don't go away.
> We'll come back another day.

When we reached home we would just sweep the sand out and I would put a clean towel over the front seat.

When we reached my Blue Datsun, there was the shining new Cadillac, perched right beside it!

The time came when the Blue Datsun began to run down, and one day she came to a dead stop.

Earlier that day she had faithfully taken me to the hospital for the 3-11 P.M. shift. My starched uniform had a clean place, and an extra hair net let the wind blow on me as I drove.

During my shift, the Blue Datsun stood forlornly in an obscure parking place, waiting, but at 11 P.M. she perked up, and we chugged home together.

Then she died! Right there in her own familiar place. Her days of being mended and patched were over — her heart had stopped beating.

That's when we hung our heads and cried over her. And then we buried her.

Yet the memories live on, and the stories will keep her in the family always.

Kathryn remembers the stories and someday she will probably write them in a book. "When I grow up, I'll be a nurse like Grammy," she has said. "When I'm too old to do anything else, I'll write books, too."

We can count on it!

Today we go to the beach in a 1984 Oldsmobile, but the trunk is covered with plastic and the seats are covered with plastic and towels—no wet bathing suits on the plush seats!

Gum wrappers go in containers and Papa's "wash your hands" keeps sticky fingers off windows. The air conditioner works and the tape recorder plays songs by Sandi Patti. And the car windows stay up.

Kathryn sits with her beach towel. Wistfully she mourns for the old days—the days of sandy buckets, dripping inner tubes and open windows with sand and wind in the air.

Finally, Kathryn finds her voice and says, "I'll never forget the Blue Datsun, Grammy. Remember the funny noises she made when we went down Oleander Drive? Everybody looked at us because it sounded like— oh, I guess I better not say what it sounded like. Anyhow, I miss her."

We laughed together!

But there was another day I didn't laugh—a day when the old Blue Datsun was still running.

I had been invited to the Country Club for lunch. The Blue Datsun chugged along, funny noises and all. At one point she stalled in the Oleander Drive traffic.

"I'll park this old relic far away so no one will see it," I thought to myself. I found a remote corner for the Blue Datsun, and joined my friends for lunch, the car forgotten.

When it was time to leave, the hostess made the remark that she had to park her new Cadillac some distance away because of the limited parking space.

"So did I," I told her.

We walked together and I wondered when she would get to her car. I didn't wonder long. When we reached my Blue Datsun, there was the shining new Cadillac, perched right beside it! I wanted to die! It didn't help a bit when I saw the absolute pity in her eyes!

From somewhere in the past I heard my Norwegian Mama say, "Pride iss a terrible thing, Margaret. Wear your high button shoes with a thankful heart."

(Those high button shoes keep coming out of the barrel of life).

"Ja, ja, Margaret, iss not so important what you have on the feet, but iss important where the feet go."[1]

Mama was right, of course, but you're right, too, Kathryn. We'll always remember the Blue Datsun.

1. *First We Have Coffee* (San Bernardin, CA: Here's Life Publishers, 1982), p. 60.

A Time to Remember

IT WAS MARCH 12, 1990. I set the table in the dining room. Violets and candles marked the occasion of Ralph's 41st birthday party. On the walls around the dining room were pictures of the family, of our 50th wedding anniversary and of our grandchildren at different ages. Birthdays are marvelous times for remembering. For thinking back. For rejoicing.

Two decades had passed since that September in 1970 when our prodigal son came home. Lena, my black friend from the college infirmary days, had wept tears of joy, exclaiming, "I done birthed my child in the Spirit."[1]

The battle to believe had been won, and amazing grace still rings across the years of time.

Twelve years had passed since our move from Greensboro to Wilmington — twelve years since Ralph had driven the Blue Datsun with yucca bushes sticking out of the windows and trunk and the infamous 100-pound troll sitting on my lap for five hours. The small house of love with its elastic walls had stretched to include a beautiful office for writing.

I browned the meat balls, Ralph's favorite, and filled a kettle with potatoes to make mashed mounds later.

"I guess I'm really Norwegian," nine-year-old Kathryn exclaimed. "I like potatoes. Sarah must be part Chinese — she just loves rice!"

I chuckled to myself. As for Eric, he was the sweet-potato boy — a real Southerner! I made sure to bake sweet potatoes for Eric.

I had given Eric long green string beans and a mound of ketchup on his plate. "Green French fries," I said.

"Grammy, I don't like cooked carrots," Eric had told me. "But I like raw carrot sticks and my favorite ranch dip."

Papa (Harold) liked creamed anything, especially cauliflower. I stirred in the cream sauce, but remembered to cut off some raw cauliflower first for Eric. He didn't like cooked vegetables at all — but chocolate cake was his real specialty.

I laughed to myself, remembering Eric in the high chair. I had given him long green string beans and a mound of ketchup on his plate. "Green French fries," I said. He ate the green beans with relish.

Shawn was unhappy. "How come Eric gets to eat string beans with his fingers and I have to use a fork?"

"Shh, Shawn. For Eric they're green French fries; for you, a big boy, they're green beans."

I mixed the ranch dip and smiled. *How I do give in to their whims,* I thought. *No one got away with such foolishness when their daddy was a boy.*

Of course it came to pass that Eric found out green beans were not green French fries, and today he eats them with a fork. By the time he grows up he'll probably like creamed cauliflower *and* cooked carrots. The years pass too quickly.

I chopped the lettuce — plain. *Oh, dear, I really shouldn't do that but the children like it plain: no cucumbers or onions or tomatoes. Catalina dressing for Sarah!*

Even that will pass and they will order tossed salad, just like their mother.

Oh, yes, Harold likes the sweet dressing — orange juice, sugar, cream and mayonnaise. He might be 78 — but some things don't pass.

When Chad comes in the summer, I'll have to remember his favorite — Norwegian pancakes! Heather, like Kathryn, is the mashed-potato and fried-chicken enthusiast.

The best part of all is when their Papa takes them out to a real Southern breakfast.

The slamming of car doors announced the arrival of the birthday boy — all 6 feet 6 inches and 200 pounds of him! The red jeep empties out two six-foot boys: Shawn, 17 years old, and Eric, 14.

"Look Grammy — my first big-girl dress!" Eleven-year-old Sarah swirled around in a long-waisted dress, trimmed with a bright scarf draped over her shoulder. Soft curls framed her gentle face.

Nine-year-old Kathryn gladly surrendered her "Sunday dress" for shorts and a top; then turned her cartwheels — just to show Papa. Growing up held little charm for her.

Chris came bouncing in with a special ice cream cake, decorated with a fisherman hauling in a line. The smiling fish was cutting bait. Chris knew her fisherman husband would like that cake.

Birthday candles, presents and cards mingled with the joy of living. Teasing, old jokes, laughter, and bubbling conversation with everyone talking at once and no one listening to anything. But everyone enjoys it all — a part of the joy of life.

As I looked across the table at Ralph, the words "the gift of God is life" came to me.

Two decades had brought so many changes!

Ralph read one of his birthday cards: "If I had a choice between a million dollars or the best dad in the world — I'd choose the million dollars. We already have the best dad in the world."

This "dad" was the one who thought he could follow the crowd of the sixties — and found out the wages weren't good, for "The wages of sin is death."

Twenty years later he is the dad who spends time with his boys — fishing, hunting and sports. This is the "rebel" who holds his girls close and tells them they are the most beautiful in the world — the smartest, the best, the greatest! Any boy coming along will have trouble following that act.

Twenty years ago this was the non-conformist who easily could have pitched a tent and lived in the woods. Today he values tradition: a commitment to marriage and family, and a love and respect for Chris, God's gift to him and to our family. He is a loving disciplinarian to his four children — and, joy of joys, he is their best friend.

The gift of God is life!

---

*I had to go back and remember
a long ago time.
Our grandchildren needed to know.*

The non-conformist style of another day — of long hair and bare feet — has long since been replaced with dignity and beauty, not only in living, but also in the creative gift of making 18th-century furniture to grace traditional homes.

My heart was full! The party was over, dishes done, wrapping paper discarded, and hugs and kisses for the birthday son, husband and father were given. The car doors slammed, the horn honked a goodbye — and the house was quiet.

Harold locked the door and put on the night lights, and we slipped quietly into bed. A busy day had come to a close.

"What a boy! What a boy!" Harold's love was special for the boy who almost lost his way. God found him and brought him home. What Ralph would have missed if he had stayed on the wrong road!

"We never know what God has in store for us when we acknowledge that Jesus is the way to the Father and to His promises," Harold said. "Psalm 16 is right when it says, 'In thy presence is fulness of joy; at thy right hand there are pleasures for evermore' [verse 11].

"We are so blessed, Margaret. So blessed. Janice and Jud, with Heather and Chad—all living for God and blessing everyone around them. And to think that Ralph and his family are here so near, and all of us are in church together . . ."

I lay there quietly as Harold drifted off to sleep. "Oh God, keep them all in your loving care," I prayed.

"Amazing grace, how sweet the sound."

I laid my head on Harold's shoulder and fell fast asleep—secure in his love and God's love for us all.

But in the morning, I knew I had to go back and remember more long ago times and do more writing. Our grandchildren needed to know about the changing times that began in the sixties.

They also needed to know that God never changes.

1. *Lena* (San Bernardino, CA: Here's Life Publishers, 1985), p. 113.

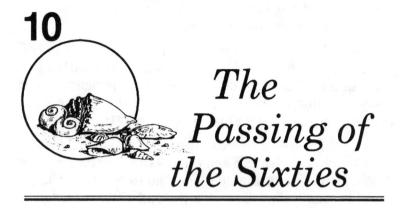

10

The Passing of the Sixties

FROM THE KITCHEN WINDOW of the college infirmary at Greensboro, Lena and I watched as the sixties passed into history. Rules in dress and conduct were changing. Young people discarded the wardrobes their parents had bought, sometimes at great sacrifice, and beautiful girls bounced around in shorts, skimpy tops, and bare feet or sandals.

Lena shook her head sadly. "When we were young we cried for dresses and shoes, and now the girls won't even wear the pretty clothes their mamas got them."

"Why do beautiful young people want to look so ugly?" I stormed.

Students often came to the infirmary choking from asthma attacks—no ban on smoking, even in classrooms. Dormitories were open for visitors.

Some young men had marched to war while others had fled. Ralph and his friends, all honor-roll students, played the devil's game and ended up as prisoners of their own war, held hostage by the enemy of man's soul without ever donning a uniform or going to a battlefield.

To them it was just a sport. Dancing to the music of a society in protest, drugs and rebellion, they were led to a far country. Rock festivals drew the youth by the thousands, lured by the desire to throw off traditional restraint.

They had their moments — a weekend here and a few days there — to remember forever.

The young beat a path to a discordant world,
trying to bring peace, love,
flowers and music. Eventually,
many of them beat a path to Lena.

From those "memorable" moments emerged horror stories of disillusionment, disease and death, and the stories ended in bitterness and a deeper rebellion. Somehow the whole world was to blame. No one wanted to come to grips with personal decisions.

Their complaints were endless. "Political systems need changing." "Church is such a bore." "Christians are hypocrites."

The young beat a path to a discordant world, trying to bring peace, love, flowers and music. Eventually, many of them beat a path to Lena. "Lord, have mercy, child! You-all fixin' to change the world and got no sense how to eat proper food. Either you come to the infirmary for Milk of Magnesia for the constipation or Kaopectate for the diarrhea." Lena shook her head.

The dreams of the young men became nightmares; peace became oblivion in a stupor of drugs; love became sexual involvement without commitment. The flower children were wilting.

While young men fought in Vietnam, the protest movement mounted; college dropouts moved into hippie communes.

Parents, who were a part of World War II and the following materialistic boom, suddenly found their homes broken — parents and children moving in opposite directions trying to find meaning to life. The wages of sin is death — death to dreams, to security, to stability and to love, and death to the soul.

On November 22, 1963, the newspaper headlines had screamed! "Sniper Kills President Kennedy in Dallas!" John F. Kennedy, 36th President of the United States of America, had been shot to death by a hidden assassin armed with a high-powered rifle.

The world mourned.

On July 31, 1964, more headlines. "Ranger 7 Successful." First closeup pictures of the moon, more than 4,000 of them, poured back to earth.

Lena and I looked out over the campus one day early in January 1970. Other headlines from the past paraded before us — February 1962: "John Glenn, First Man in Space." June 1963: "First Woman in Space." Great scientific explorations were quickly covering the earth with knowledge.

Success one place, tragedy another. Death and tragedy had resulted from a desperately wicked heart, a heart only God can know. Man's scientific knowledge can't reach the depths of man's sin. Only the power of God can change the heart. *The wages of sin is death — but the gift of God is eternal life.* Man chooses: death or life.

"Looks like knowledge fillin' the earth, but wisdom gettin' left behind," Lena said. "The Lord says, 'The fear of the LORD is the beginning of wisdom' [Proverbs 9:10]. Man walks in space; me, I walks with the Lord."

The rebellious youth came, in their bare feet and long hair, to find Jesus.

"One small step for man; one giant step for mankind," and Neil Armstrong had pressed his left foot into moon dust at 10:56 P.M., July 19, 1969.

Edwin Eugene Aldrin, Jr. stepped onto the surface twenty minutes later, exclaiming, "Beautiful! Beautiful! Beautiful! A magnificent desolation."

At 11:42 P.M. they unfurled the Stars and Stripes and the flag stood in the airless, windless atmosphere of the moon, held taut by a rod along the top.

One astronaut stood back and saluted.

"This has to be the most historic telephone call ever made," President Nixon said to them. "I just can't tell you how proud I am. Because of what you have done the heavens have become part of man's world. As you talk to us from the Sea of Tranquility, it inspires us to redouble our efforts to bring peace and tranquility to man."

The next day, Sunday, President Nixon and leaders of the nation prayed and worshiped in the White House, their thoughts fixed on space. Frank Borman, Commander of the Apollo 8 space voyage, read Genesis 1:1-10 during the morning service.

Across the world there were prayers for peace. But a picture of a G.I. wading through the Mekong Delta and listening to the news on radio made us realize how far from peace we were.

Across the world Christians from all denominations were crying out to God for a spiritual revival in the world. "Lord, send the old time power. We need Your power to be witnesses to the ends of the earth," they pleaded.

Ralph's friends began to come — to see what had happened to turn the rebel into a traditional married man.

Prayer meetings seemed to mushroom around the country. The rebellious youth saw the reality of true Christianity and came, in their bare feet and long hair, to find Jesus — the truth, the life, the way.

The Jesus people came, even in their non-conformist manner, with their message of God's love. Young and old met together in homes where love asked no questions and rebellious hearts of stone turned to the God of love who reached out with open arms.

Guitars strummed while the non-conformist and the white-haired traditionalist sang together, "Jesus loves me! This I know . . . "

Into the seventies these young people came. Not ready for the traditional churches they had left behind, they gathered in house meetings and witnessed of God's love in their own way.

Into the seventies came our Ralph, transformed by the power of God! Our friend, Mr. Mason, the white-haired patriarch, never gave up. His arms opened wide. Shortly after that, wedding bells mingled with Christmas chimes to announce to the world the marriage of Christine Fisher and Ralph Jensen.

Then Ralph's friends began to come—to see what had happened to turn the rebel into a traditional married man.

They came "as is." God made them "as His."

11

Jeremiah
— the Raccoon

Keith and Kevin, brothers, were two who came to our home in Greensboro to see what had happened to Ralph. There they stood — cut-off jeans, sandaled feet, beards and long blond hair and vacant blue eyes — and a tiny raccoon on Keith's shoulder . . .

A raccoon!?

"Hi. This is Jeremiah," Keith said to me. "I found him in the woods, and it's up to me to keep him alive." Keith's dull blue eyes stared into space.

"Oh, I see," I answered.

I didn't see, but Ralph warned me that Keith's mind was strung out on drugs and that Keith believed his mission in life was to care for the baby raccoon whose mother had died.

"Where shall we put Jeremiah?" I asked.

"Oh, he stays with me."

We sat around the dining room table and Harold asked the blessing — with one eye on Jeremiah still sitting on Keith's shoulder.

We passed the meatballs and mashed potatoes, standard fare at the Jensens', while Keith fed Jeremiah from a doll's bottle filled with milk.

I had been warned to "play it cool" — drugs did strange things to young people.

When they came to our door with vacant eyes, I just hugged them, then fed them. Words couldn't be heard anymore. They knew some of the words, the Scriptures, the admonitions. They had memorized Bible verses in Sunday school and had heard enough preaching to convert the world.

Ralph taught me well. "They only understand love, Mom — that's all."

Did love include a raccoon? I had to learn to love Jeremiah. When I found "marks" on my carpet I bit my lip — and scrubbed. I almost lost my cool when I put my foot into a wet shoe! Ugh!!

Jeremiah even slept with Keith. I prayed a lot!

Dan, our older son, showed the boys the farm, and together they cut down brush, washed up in the cool mountain spring, bunked in the cabin, and pitched in with the building of the Shalom Valley chalet.

My faithful Blue Datsun carried a trunkful of food to Shalom Valley. We camped and picnicked there, and the guitars strummed into the night.

Jeremiah found a home and became a favorite pet. Eventually even the dogs tolerated him.

In the hot summer when I gardened in shorts and a sleeveless top, Jeremiah would sneak up behind me and climb to my shoulder. His cold finger-like paws climbing up my bare legs sent chills up my spine. One day I scolded him. "Jeremiah, you should be ashamed, scaring me to pieces like that."

Jeremiah looked at me and talked back, "Brrrr."

I asked, "What do you want?"

He jumped down and ran over to a large tin that contained marshmallows.

"Now Jeremiah, you know those are for a wiener and marshmallow roast tonight. You should be ashamed, eating my marshmallows."

We took care of the outside while God, by His Spirit, worked on the inside.

He cocked his head and with his little "Brrrr," almost said, "Please?"

I yielded and tossed him a fat marshmallow. He looked at me, gave me a quick "Brrrr" thank you and ran to the creek.

That's when I forgave him for all the wet shoes and spots on the rug.

Keith and Kevin were getting brown in the sun, eating, sleeping, and loving the land. Their expressions were no longer vacant.

Even now, these many years later, I can hear the whippoorwill, see the stars over the valley, and smell the hot dogs and marshmallows at the open fire. I can still picture Keith strumming his guitar and hear his plaintive songs winging into the night.

Another young man, Rob, handsome like Michelangelo's *David*, with dark curly hair and soccer muscles, came with bitterness and anger. Gradually God's Spirit worked on the inside while we opened our arms on the outside. The bitterness left and love replaced the anger. Rob became a new creature in Christ.

Back then we spared the words and lavished the love. God was at work.

On Tuesday nights we beat a path to the Mason's prayer meeting. Young people sat on the floor and the music flowed into the streets. They came to see what happened to Ralph — and stayed for six months. We took care of the outside — God's Spirit worked on the inside.

At one large meeting, where the young people were telling about God's love for them, a sweet old lady came up to me. "Well, I never!" she declared.

I had a feeling that her *never* meant that *I* never should have done it — opened my home to barefoot, bearded boys, melancholy music and a raccoon. I had a feeling she thought we had fallen short of evangelism and taken leave of our senses.

So I tried to explain why I sometimes stayed home from church to do household chores. "You see, someone else picks the young people up and takes them to the meetings, and I wash the dishes. No, I don't have a dishwasher. Then I scrub the kitchen (Jeremiah, you know) and then I empty the garbage."

Wide-eyed, she was shaking her head now. I went on. "All this time the washing machine is doing one load of clothes after another." The more she frowned, the more I tried to explain. "I pray while I work and the Lord and I just work it all out together."

She smiled patiently at me, and I continued, "He said, 'It's okay, Margaret. When you do it for them, you do it for Me.'

"You see, someone has to clean the toilets while someone else shows the way — God's way."

"Well, I never heard such a gospel!" She walked off and I'm sure she put me on someone's prayer list. Oh, well, I need all the help I can get.

I dried my hands and brushed back my stringy hair, but I couldn't stop the tears. I was angry.

Late one Saturday night I was all alone. Harold was out of town and everyone else had gone to a prayer meeting. I was scrubbing the kitchen floor on my hands and knees. (My Norwegian mama never believed in mops. She's in heaven now — and I do use a mop now and then.)

I had been to the grocery and used practically all my meager paycheck for the boys' groceries. While I was scrubbing, I mentally figured my bank balance and realized I was overdrawn $50! Everything wrong happens when Harold is away.

I fell apart! It's strange how we brace ourselves for the great calamities of life but often fall apart at some small crisis. Right then $50 seemed to me like an unscalable mountain.

I slammed the scrub brush on the floor and cried into my bucket of sudsy water. "It's not fair, Lord. It's just not fair. All I do is work, cook, scrub and take these kids no one wants and then I make a mistake — fifty lousy dollars! It's just not fair!"

I had a good cry as I finished the floor and emptied the bucket of water. I dried my hands and brushed back my stringy hair, but I couldn't stop the tears. I was angry. "Don't you care, Lord?" Just then the doorbell rang.

"Oh, no. Somebody's kid needs a place to sleep! I don't want to see anyone. I'm too upset."

I took a deep breath and went to the door. There stood our friend, Bob Adams.

"Margaret, I was at the meeting with all the hippies and the Lord spoke to me and said, 'Go, give Margaret $50 for groceries.' "

I didn't answer. I just stood there with my mouth open as he told this story.

"She surely doesn't need $50. Besides, Lord, I'm in a meeting."

"Go! Now!"

"Yes, Lord!"

I finally found my voice. "Oh, Bob — I'm overdrawn $50. Harold is gone and he'd be disturbed if my check bounced. I was convinced God had forgotten me."

We rejoiced together. Bob had obeyed and I had been shown God's care for His weary child.

I was reminded of how we are all overdrawn at times, not always $50, but sometimes we find ourselves short of faith, creativity, hope or courage. We feel empty, alone and in despair, with simply nothing in our account to draw from–overdrawn in energy, strength or the ability to know how to put one foot ahead of the other. Someone once cried on my shoulder, "I am not a victorious Christian — I am just surviving." That's the way we feel.

Then, in those darkest hours, God's messenger comes: a friend with $50, or someone with a song, or we read or hear a Bible verse, or feel the warm clasp of a hand that strengthens, or hear a word of hope, or even receive just a smile or a hug from someone — just enough to enable us to take one more step. The old song comes to mind: "Just when I need Him, Jesus is near." It is really true. Jesus never fails.

Fifty dollars wasn't the only blessing that night. Before they came home, Keith and Kevin each experienced God's transforming power through His amazing grace. "Great Is Thy Faithfulness" became Keith's theme song.

Come to think of it — it is mine, also.

12

Surprise Visits

IT WAS A QUIET EVENING. Supper dishes were done and the young people were sitting on the floor in the den listening to tapes.

They hungered for God's Word and drank in the messages and testimonies of other young Christians. Contemporary Christian music was replacing the rock and roll of another day.

Ralph slipped out of the group, went to the piano in the front room, and began softly playing an old song, "No One Understands Like Jesus."

He turned and saw a face pressed against the doorway glass—a familiar face from another time in New York. He jumped up and quickly pulled the door open.

"Billy, you old rascal!" Ralph said. "How in the world did you get here? Come on in!"

Billy, an old friend of Ralph's from college days, was in shock. "I came to look you up. Look at you—a square, and playing a hymn! You've got to be kidding!"

"Come on, come in and meet the gang. You remember Rob and Kevin don't you? By the way, how did you find me?"

"I was in High Point [a neighboring town] and I asked a stranger, 'Do you know where Ralph Jensen lives?' 'Yeah, he lives in Greensboro—I know exactly where it is,' this guy told me. He brought me here." Billy shook his head in disbelief and continued, "That really blew me away—a stranger in another town! Wow!"

"Come on in," Ralph urged. "We're listening to a tape in the den."

Billy slipped into a corner—as far away as possible—and then crawled under a table.

Everyone who was listening to the tape heard the voice urge, "Fall on your face before God and ask His forgiveness."

They all started to pray, and Billy crawled out from under the table and cried out to God for forgiveness. Like a child he received God's gift of eternal salvation.

A few days later Billy attended a wedding in Winston Salem, then returned with the newlyweds. "I told them they couldn't go on their honeymoon until they got right with God."

They did!

When Billy returned to New York he met an old friend who had just returned from Vietnam.

"Hey, Billy! What's new? Anything besides sex, drugs and liquor?"

"I'll tell you what's new—God!"

"God?" Tony asked.

"Yeah, God!" Billy told him.

"I'm bored, Billy—bored! Since I came home Pa said, 'Go to Mass with your mama. All the time you in the war, your mama she go to church and pray. So, Tony, go to Mass with Mama—that's the best thing you can do.'"

"So, Billy, where's God?"

"In North Carolina."

"No kidding? No wonder I didn't find Him in church. He left New York already."

"'Sure, Pa, sure,' I told him. So I did, and I'm bored. Poor Ma—so happy to have me home, but I'm plain bored. So, Billy, where's God?"

"In North Carolina."

"No kidding? No wonder I didn't find Him in church. He left New York already. Can't say I blame Him. I'd like to leave, too. Carolina? No kidding? So, maybe I should go with you—just for kicks."

"Come on, Tony. Go back with me."

"I'll see. Ma won't like it, and Pa says, 'Keep your mama happy—the least you can do.'"

And so Tony (can't remember his real name) told his father he'd like to go to North Carolina.

"What for?" his father asked.

"To find God!"

"You mean to tell me that, in a city like New York, filled with churches, and your mama going to Mass all the time, you can't find God? Hey, Tony, if you can't find God in New York, forget it! Can't blame you for leaving New York — but why North Carolina? You go to Mass with your mama — can't stand to see her cry no more — forget North Carolina."

Tony forgot — for a little while. Then one night he was awakened with a deep desire to pray, and he knelt down and cried out to God wherever He was.

In walked three bushy-haired young men and a girl with long, stringy hair. With the group came a cat. A cat?!

Quietly he slipped out of bed and awakened his mother, "Ma, I've got to go to North Carolina. I've got to find God."

She patted his cheek. "So go, already. Go, and I pray — but don't wake up your pa."

The day came when Billy and Tony arrived at Bethel Spring Dale.

God found Tony!

For days the old gang rejoiced together, and sure enough, when Tony returned to New York he found God was even in New York. He was in Tony's heart.

Others came to Bethel Spring Dale, too.

One time, it was midnight in Greensboro. Lights were dim, doors were locked, and we were ready for bed when into the driveway came the headlights of a van bearing a California license plate.

"Is this Ralph Jensen's home?" one young man asked. "We were told we could come here for food and sleep."

"Certainly! Come on in!" I stifled a yawn.

In walked three bushy-haired young men and a girl with long, stringy hair. She looked frail and full of fear. With the group came a cat.

A cat!? The memory of Jeremiah was all too vivid.

The cat looked at me with a haughty expression that said, "Of course, I'm a cat." She sat down in a corner to watch us.

I heated the kettle of homemade soup and sliced a loaf of my homemade bread. They ate like it was their last meal. I opened a can of peaches and sliced the famous Lena poundcake we managed to keep on hand.

I took the boys upstairs where three clean beds were ready. They looked at the clean sheets and asked to take showers.

"Of course!" Why not? The sun wasn't up yet.

I took the young girl to Jan's old room. Pictures of Jan lined the wall—a bald baby, mischievous lovable first grader, high school, college and wedding pictures.

I laid one of Jan's nightgowns and a robe across the bed. On a shelf was a much-loved Madame Alexander doll.

"Keep my room the same, Mom," Jan always told me. I understood. We all need a place to come home to. (Jud doesn't mind the frills—he knows his Jan.)

The frail girl stood in front of the wedding picture. I saw tears on her cheeks—and I wondered, *Is she pregnant?* I kept quiet.

"I'm going to my aunt. The boys gave me a ride." (Now I was sure.)

She smiled sadly, "I think I'll take a shower."

Later, when she curled up like a kitten in Jan's bed, I sat beside her and stroked her damp hair. I just sat there loving her without words.

Then I prayed, committing her to God's loving care. I kissed her goodnight and turned out the light. It was so difficult not to preach. I had to trust God's Spirit to work on the inside while I worked on the outside. Within moments she was asleep.

When I went upstairs the boys were in their clean beds. I sat for a moment on each bed, stroking damp hair, and praying over the boy in the bed. Then I kissed each one good night—"Just like I do all my boys," I told them.

The smell of bacon and coffee brought them all to life in the morning. Even the cat got fed. Soon they were off in the van after a hug, a goodbye and a God-bless-you. The van slipped around the bend, and they were gone.

I don't remember their names and I never heard from them again, but God knew who they were and I believed the time would come when their hearts would turn toward home.

It was difficult for me to let them go. They were someone's children, and probably someone was praying for them. "Love, Mom, don't preach," Ralph had said.

"Lots of these kids could preach better sermons than most preachers I've heard. They know the words, but only the Holy Spirit can speak so they can hear."

I knew Ralph was right, but I always thought that if I could be convincing enough, they would hear. I learned to trust God's Holy Spirit to guide me as to when to speak. I also realized that most of the time He just uses unconditional love. Our voices sometimes drown out what God is saying. Love, food and shelter opens the heart, and perhaps, down the road, someone else will be led to say what the heart can hear. Then God will do what we can't do.

One night Ralph picked up two Navy boys who were A.W.O.L. When they reached our house, Ralph said, "They have no place to stay, Mom — and they're hungry!"

The gang was there — Kevin, Keith, Rob, Billy, and the rest — and the dining room rang with laughter and jokes.

One of the Navy boys sat in a corner. "Hey, man," he whispered to his friend, "these people are on drugs. The food is spiked and I'm not eating."

The two sailors huddled together, glad to be out of the cold, but afraid of what they were into. They drank water from the faucet. They eyed the food hungrily, but refused to eat. We had learned to leave "as is" alone and ask no questions.

During the evening we called our friend Bob Adams, an old Navy man, and when he arrived we introduced him to the boys. They bolted for the door. A Navy man to pull them in!

Bob grabbed them, "Hey, man, let me tell you about when I went A.W.O.L. Believe me, you guys can't top the trouble I was into when I was in the Navy."

They watched wide-eyed as Bob related, "I was really rebellious—and daring! One day we were going somewhere on a train, and we decided to have a party. We had what we thought was a great time, and we all proceeded to get drunk. Among the other crazy things we did, just for a lark, my buddies hung me out the train window! It was a miracle they didn't let go of my feet . . . talk about trouble—I was it!

"Then one day I met Jesus. He changed my life and the old things went away, and God forgave me my sin and gave me a new life." He glanced around the room, then looked back at the two sailors. "You see these folks? So happy? That's why they are so happy. Jesus set them free.

"Now tell me, when is the last time you saw a happy, crazy bunch like this, not drunk and no drugs?"

The Navy boys were a study. Fear? Wonder? Longing? Bob recognized the hunger of the heart.

At midnight they knelt together and the Navy boys weren't A.W.O.L. from God anymore. They turned themselves in to Him, and He took them into His heart of love.

"Man, we're starved!" they admitted at last. Out came the food, and they ate with relish.

"Tomorrow, I'll go with you to your officer and we'll get the whole thing straightened out," Bob offered.

The boys slept soundly, and when breakfast came they devoured bacon and eggs. Then they were gone. The heart hunger had been met as well as the physical hunger.

Never did get their names, but that's all right; God wrote them down in His Book of Life.

13

Out of the Seventies

THE MASON PRAYER MEETING was crowded with old and young. Some sat on the stairs, or on the kitchen floor and in the halls. The old folks and visitors had chairs. I had a chair and I wasn't a visitor.

I sat beside two visitors, a strong, handsome black-bearded youth and a gentle girl. The music filled the house and street.

White-haired Mr. Mason spoke of God's love—he never condemned and he always reassured his listeners that God waits with open arms. "Tonight I know there is someone God is speaking to—it's time to come home!"

Ralph and Chris were there. Kevin and Keith rejoiced in God's love. Sandy, Judy and Lisa joined Billy and Rob in praises to God.

I looked over at "my family" and marveled at the grace of God. Bob Adams, our Navy friend, was there, playing his clarinet, and ready to pray with anyone in need.

I sat beside my two strangers.

The piano bench was called the *hot seat* because it was the only available space to kneel and pray. Tears covered that hot seat as young and old had knelt at the bench to weep out their repentance and receive God's grace—His love and forgiveness.

No sin was too deep. God's love could reach the lowest depths and bring a repentant one to the heights of peace and joy.

"There is someone who needs Jesus tonight," Mr. Mason urged gently, compassionately.

I heard a stirring beside me. My black-bearded friend looked at me, "Come with me to the bench." I took his hand and as we eased out of the crowded seating, the young girl grabbed my other hand. "Don't leave me," she cried.

Together we went to the hot seat. Mr. Mason prayed with them as they surrendered their lives to follow Jesus. As we knelt together I never dreamed what God had in store for these two young people—Jack and Adrian.

Through business friends I was able to get work for these two new Christians, and the discipline of work, Christian fellowship, Bible study and prayer allowed them to grow in wisdom and understanding.

One day I was baking cookies when Jack burst into the kitchen. "Mom, I don't understand it, but I just feel the need to go back to school. Some friends said, though, that I needed the discipline of work. After all, Adrian and I just got married. What do you think?"

I took the cookies out of the oven and as fast as I took them off the cookie sheet, Jack ate them, and washed them down with a glass of milk.

I prayed quietly, "Please, Lord, guide Jack Your way."

Then I knew, deep inside, Jack should go to school. "I think it's schooltime," I told him.

Their children are growing up, fluent in Spanish. Perhaps they will have an impact on our increasing Spanish population.

We hugged, laughed, prayed, and asked for God's guidance as to finances. At the prayer meeting, God's precious people surrounded Jack and Adrian with love and prayer as they ventured out of the boat to walk on water.

They went to Montreat, North Carolina, Jack to school and Adrian to work. Godly people invited this special young couple to give their testimony in churches. They excelled in every venture of faith, school and witnessing.

Like Abraham of old, they left security behind and ventured to Mexico as missionaries. They became fluent in Spanish, and Jack's Latin appearance made him "one of them."

Miraculously, a van for travel was supplied, and every need was met. Today — because of their ministry — hundreds of people are in churches and a number of young people are being trained in Bible school.

Because of Jack and Adrian's witness, others followed, and eventually Kevin and his beautiful wife Susan left it all behind and went to Mexico, too.

Others followed on short-term missions, to build, to teach, to show forth God's love.

We took them "as is." God made them "as His."

The missionary work of these young people, the miracles they saw, the roads they traveled by plane or van could fill a book—but that is their story to tell.

Their children are growing up, fluent in Spanish and understanding other cultures. Perhaps they will have an impact on our increasing Spanish population. God is getting them ready ahead of time!

Mr. Mason is at home with the Lord, but his legacy of love remains forever.

A policeman stopped me and looked at this white-haired old lady with these noisy boys. "What is going on here?" he demanded.

For everything there is a season, and the early seventies was the time for "my children" to wend their weary footsteps to 103 Bethel Spring Dale in Greensboro.

Our patient neighbors put up with vans, motorcycles, cookouts, singing and noise. Our garbage was filled with unmentionable junk, and I dreaded a police search in our respectable part of town.

One day a neighbor came in. "What's going on in this house?" he asked.

I trembled. *Now we are in trouble,* I thought, *with all the noise, disturbing the peace and the garbage can — whew!* I stammered out something about Ralph's friends. (Oh, horrors. That sounded even worse. He knew Ralph — when??)

"The reason I ask," he said, as tears filled his eyes, "I need what these kids have."

We prayed together.

One night I had my Blue Datsun filled with happy young people, singing and noisy.

A policeman stopped me and looked at this white-haired old lady with these noisy boys. "What is going on here?" he demanded. "Have you been drinking?"

"I stick to coffee!" I assured him. He didn't think it was funny. "We are on our way to a prayer meeting," I ventured. That was worse.

"You are what?" he roared.

"Oh, yes, sir, we are on our way to a prayer meeting. These kids are really happy."

Everyone burst out laughing — it sounded so ridiculous.

He eyed me carefully, checked my driver's license and muttered, "Now I've heard everything! A prayer meeting! Well, you'd better get going!"

We watched him scratch his head. I know he heard us singing, "I'm so glad Jesus set us free."

He could take that one any way he wanted to.

14

The Wedding

JANUARY 15, 1973. Keith was getting married in a few days.

What meant so much to me was meeting Kevin and Keith's parents. The mother, a warm, plump farmer's wife, hugged me. With tears streaming down her cheeks, she turned to her stoic German husband and said, "This is the Mama who took our children in."

His eyes moistened as he shook hands with me. "Thank you . . . "

We couldn't speak.

Later that night the doorbell rang and there stood Ralph, Chris and baby Shawn. "Hi. We came to spend the night, and besides we don't have homemade cinnamon rolls for breakfast. Can't stand to miss anything. With Dan and Rob here, we can all go to church together."

Chris and I prepared food and the men huddled together to talk "farm." What a family! I love it!

You'll never guess what happened. The next morning I stayed home to prepare a roast for the gang and take care of Shawn. The men, laughing and talking (and full of coffee and cinnamon rolls) piled into the car to go to church — and *forgot Chris!*

I said, "Chris, this is the time to pack your bag and go home to your mother!"

"Forget it," she announced. "I'm staying with you."

The college president sat in one row; jean-clad youth with dull boots and long hair, from another generation, sat in another.

You should have seen those four sheepish men when they returned from church, all mumbling their apologies. Chris said, "It's good to have something to hold over your heads."

She's one in a million!

On the Saturday evening of Keith and Barbara's wedding, a blanket of snow covered the quiet college campus, but the candlelit chapel invited the guests into its warmth.

The college president sat in one row; jean-clad youth with dull boots and long hair, from another generation, sat in another. Fur-wrapped, bejeweled women of society walked down the aisle on the arms of lanky youths (who looked a little out of place in their tuxedos) to be seated with the other guests.

Warm, friendly faces of the Pennsylvania farmers nodded and smiled to young and old as they, too, joined the other wedding guests.

Dignified Hunter Dalton, owner of the Snow Lumber Co., took his place. He had given the "hippies" jobs — with some persuasion from his beautiful mother, Frances Dalton. Frances loved "my boys," and Hunter never regretted his decision — he came to love my boys too.

Businessmen, musicians, a nightclub entertainer, the settled elite of the establishment and those from the country and town, young and old, filled the pews of the college chapel that snowy night.

To me it was beautiful — flowers and candles, and an array of informal youths, some hidden behind palms. Ken Helser's music came softly — guitars strumming to the slow, gentle beat of drums and whispering overtones of the organ. The sound was like the sighing of wind through tall pines, or like waves rolling on a sandy shore.

The ministers stood in their places. Then came Keith the groom, and Kevin the best man, dressed in tuxedos — tall and smiling.

I reached for my evening bag and grabbed a lacy frill to dab at the tears stealing down my cheeks.

Harold nudged me — and offered me a mint.

These were "my boys," boys who had come to me with bare feet, cut-off jeans, beards and long hair — and a raccoon named Jeremiah. They had blank stares and hollow eyes then.

Through my tears I watched my own Ralph, tall and confident, escorting Sandy, Keith's sister. Her long dark hair fell softly against the back of her green velvet gown. Her life, too, had been made new. Lisa, blonde and fair, her face sparkling with joy, stood next to Rob, the once bitter young man, now so gentle and full of love.

The music swelled and the words rang out as a slim young girl stepped to the microphone and sang a love song to Jesus:

> *I'll never be able to pay the debt I owe.*
> *It was paid long ago*
> *By Jesus' own precious blood.*

My lace handkerchief was soaked. I needed a box of Kleenex. Harold reluctantly released his pocket handkerchief.

Voices blended as the congregation sang,

> *There's a sweet, sweet spirit in this place;*
> *And I know that it's the Spirit of the Lord.*

The candlelight fell on faces: ruddy lined faces, fresh from the farm; young faces filled with love; dignified men; others misty-eyed and humble.

The groom's mother and father reflected thanks to God since five of their children had been changed in that wonderful summer.

The music swelled, the organ pealed, drums rolled, guitars burst into waves and the trumpet sounded as Barbara came gracefully down the aisle — beautiful in a white satin gown and flowing veil. Her soft brown hair framed her lovely face, and her large eyes were filled with love and tears as she looked at Keith.

Then came the words, "Dearly beloved, we are gathered here . . . " (Oh, God, how we are gathered here — New York, Pennsylvania, Massachusetts, Maryland, the

Carolinas . . .). The ceremony continued. "I now pronounce you man and wife."

Communion followed. "This is My body . . . this is My blood . . . for you."

Then the pastor announced, "The bride and groom have requested that anyone who wishes to join them in prayer may come to the altar."

The pews emptied. After the prayer, the guests quietly returned to their seats.

"Thank You, Father, for hearing Your children," I whispered.

"I want to sing my song for you . . .

> *Great is Thy faithfulness,*
> *O God my Father . . . "*

That was when I broke down and wept.

Softly a soloist sang,

> O happy day that fixed my choice
> On Thee my Savior and my God!

The bride and groom, hand in hand, walked down the aisle swinging to the song's upbeat tempo.

> Happy day, happy day,
> When Jesus washed my sins away!

The guests followed, also singing, *"O happy day!"*

* * *

Two short years later, the wind blew cold over the tombstones of the village cemetery.

Once again we gathered from the East and West, young and old, furs and army coats. The college chapel filled with mourners. "Dust to dust. Ashes to ashes . . . Our beloved Keith is home with Jesus."

One by one, they stood to tell of Keith's shining faith, full of the love of Jesus—only three short years—the same amount of time for ministry that Jesus had!

Keith, the outdoorsman who loved animals, had cared for famous racing horses owned by a neurosurgeon. One day Keith fainted. The cautious eye of the surgeon made the diagnosis after tests: a brain tumor. Keith survived the surgery four months, then God had taken him home suddenly.

Beautiful Barbara stood by the flower-draped casket and smiled through her tears, "Keith saw Jesus just before he died—then Jesus took him home."

They played a tape of Keith's voice, out of the past, telling of his love for Jesus.

"I want to sing my song for you . . .

Great is Thy faithfulness,
O God my Father . . . "

That was when I broke down and wept, remembering. Night after night, when Keith couldn't sleep, he used to strum his guitar and play, "Great Is Thy Faithfulness." God had reached down from glory and taken Keith home. In faithfulness. In love.

I wondered what would happen to lovely, gentle Barbara. Slender and graceful, that day she moved among family and friends bringing faith and comfort to others. Several years later she remarried.

I have that tape, and whenever I listen to it, I'm impressed again with God's great faithfulness.

For everything there is a season. The non-conformists, called "my boys," were returning to school, getting established in the market place, beginning their own families—and settling back into the traditional churches. Then they began bringing new life to others, life without legalism or the bondage of powerless tradition.

"For I am not ashamed of the gospel of Christ" (Romans 1:16) became their theme; the method of sharing their faith was through unconditional love.

One day Kevin, neat and trim, was in the post office when an unkempt, barefoot hippy walked in.

When the young man left, an irate woman shuddered, "Ugh, I hate hippies!"

Kevin turned quietly and faced her. "Do you know that God loves hippies? That's how my brother and I were until Jesus changed us. Now he's at home with the Lord."

The post office became quiet, and tears of remorse stung the haughty cheeks.

Finally, the house on Bethel Spring Dale became quiet again and there was time to enjoy the family and the beauty around us. During my long walks around Lake Hamilton, I pondered events that had piled on top of each other, and I marveled at the grace of God.

We watched the young families grow in wisdom and in understanding. Although separated—sometimes by miles, sometimes by death—love drew us close. We would all meet at the throne of grace. "Great is Thy faithfulness, O God!"

Then the silence was broken!

15

No Soy Sauce on Ice Cream!

IT WAS JULY 1975 when the plane, on its last lap of the journey from Asia, slipped out from behind the clouds and made a gentle landing at the Greensboro Airport.

Stan and Ginny Smith, missionaries from Vietnam, watched with us as Pastor An, a Vietnamese pastor, and his family stepped out of the plane. Their two teenage boys were swallowed up in Navy coats, and the mother held her two daughters closely as they came toward us.

I was touched by their weariness, their gaunt expressions. When they saw the Smiths, though, hope rose in their faces and their eyes brightened.

A tearful reunion made us realize how dear these people were to the missionaries — and how much all had suffered.

As a family we had watched the tragic news of the fall of Vietnam and Dan had wondered about the fate of the veteran missionaries, Gordon and Laura Smith.

"I wonder if they made it to safety," Dan had said. "I'll never forget their visit with me in the Da Nang Hospital." Just before being shipped out he'd had a severe kidney infection. He later learned that most of his company died in battle.

A phone call to the United World Mission reassured us that the senior Smiths were safe at home. Their concern was for their son Stan and his wife Ginny. Stan and Ginny were among the last to leave Saigon.

Then came the pleas, "We need sponsors for two Vietnamese pastors now in U.S.A. camps."

So a council meeting of the Jensens around the dining room table resulted in our sponsoring two families, Pastor An's and Pastor Dicht's—eleven Vietnamese who spoke no English.

Pastor Dicht and his family arrived later.

In the meantime, Chris, Ralph and two-year-old Shawn, who were waiting to get into their new home, were temporarily housed with us. Into this setting Eric was born—to the delight of the Vietnamese who love children deeply.

I had been taught well by my Norwegian mama to take one day at a time—more often, one hour at a time. Mama's home had been filled with Norwegian immigrants—but she shared their language and culture. We Jensens had another language, and a different culture from these Vietnamese families.

Chris set up classes for English lessons. Harold found work for the men, and the women were introduced to American housekeeping. Vietnamese words and English words posted on the refrigerator kept up the limited communication. The children knew no barriers and they played together easily.

Pastor Roy Putnam of Trinity Church not only opened his heart, but he also opened the doors of the church for Christian fellowship. The response of this wonderful church provided housing for the Vietnamese missionaries; it also provided love and understanding to help bind up the wounds of broken dreams. Everything had been left behind, including the two ministers' churches, Bible schools, and orphanages.

Gordon and Laura Smith had done extensive work establishing those orphanages, as well as Bible schools and churches, and a renowned medical center and clinic for lepers.

Pastor An had rescued the orphans, but he could not rescue his own children.

Gordon Smith was determined to return! "I especially want to take tapes, and other help, to the blind." He was sure the Viet Cong would recognize his lifetime of service to the people of Vietnam and allow him to return. The younger missionary, Stan Smith, knew better.

Horror stories followed, not only in the news, but also in firsthand reports from these faithful Vietnamese pastors.

Pastor An had been able to rescue more than twenty orphans in his jeep and move them through the precarious jungle. When they came to an impassable river where bridges had been destroyed, Pastor An cried out to God, "You delivered Moses; make a way for us."

An Army helicopter appeared, rescued them, and took them all to Saigon. From Saigon they were airlifted to America.

Mrs. An grieved for her three youngest children, left behind with their grandparents when the communists blocked the roads. Pastor An had rescued the orphans, but he could not rescue his own. His grief was deep.

The work and dreams of a lifetime seemed to crumble under the tyranny of the ruthless enemy. Churches, orphanages, clinics and schools were all destroyed. What a waste!

One day a hundred-pound bag of rice
was on the porch,
along with a gallon of soy sauce.
Our guests put soy sauce on everything.

The missionaries and the faithful pastors believed that, out of the ashes of ruin, God would raise up a people of faith—and He did!

The Dicht family fled the Viet Cong and managed to find safety on an enormous barge along with hundreds of others—only to be shot at by the soldiers on the shore. The ropes were cut and the overcrowded barge drifted out to sea without food or water.

Pastor Dicht was left for dead among the baggage. The mother prayed! Rain came and with it restoration of life in the father. Later an American ship rescued them.

Bit by bit we heard the stories and marveled at how these people had survived. Now they had to learn a new language and adjust to a foreign culture.

A cynical reporter asked me, "How do you expect to feed all these people?"

"Oh," I laughed, "don't you know the story of the fish and the loaves in the Bible?"

He didn't!

When I came home, someone had put a very large tuna fish in the freezer and Pillsbury Company had sent cases of bread mixes. Talk about the loaves and fishes! I thought the story too good to miss, so I wrote to the president of Pillsbury to let him know how his company was a part of a miracle. He was delighted! Everyone likes to be part of a miracle.

We saw miracles every day.

One day a hundred-pound bag of rice was on the porch, along with a gallon of soy sauce. Our guests put soy sauce on everything—toast, eggs, rice, etc. One day we made homemade ice cream and I announced, "No soy sauce on ice cream! American tradition!"

That settled it.

Trips to the mall were hilarious, especially when the dignified men bowed to the mannequins and said, "Good morning."

Dr. James Bruce gave free physicals. English classes were offered—along with tutoring service. Businessmen from Trinity Church offered work. We kept a shuttle service going: doctor, English classes, work and church.

Janice, our daughter, flew down from Boston to help with household chores, and she offered some good advice, "Let the women cook."

They were elated! They caught fish in the lake (no one else caught fish) and they cleaned the fish in our driveway. The hose was handy.

They sat on the floor and slivered string beans or cut a chicken up in small pieces so fast I couldn't keep up with them.

Poor Harold, he had to read the newspaper — and smile — whether he liked what he was reading or not!

I watched them stir-fry one of those cut-up chickens, then add vegetables, and finally put that delicious concoction around a mountain of rice.

They must have choked on my mashed potatoes, meat balls and creamed vegetables (Norskie style).

In the meantime, Dan, and Gordon and Laura Smith, drew up plans for mobile homes on Shalom Farm. Harold purchased three air conditioned homes and our dreams soared. This would be a temporary transition period for them — time to learn the language and culture — a chance to grow their own gardens and raise chickens.

But our dreams again were changed. After the two families had been in our home four months, someone made lovely downtown apartments available to them. Their adjustment to city life was amazing. We had underestimated their ability to adapt to their new world.

The mobile homes were sold. God had a better plan.

Within a short time Laura and Gordon Smith went home to be with the Lord. How the courts of heaven must have resounded with, "Welcome home, good and faithful servants."

Stan and Ginny Smith and their lovely family went to Senegal Africa as missionaries.

Today, Pastor An is the Southeast Asian Coordinator in the Mt. Vernon Baptist Association. They live in Alexandria, Virginia.

After years of prayer and working through various organizations, and by means of negotiations and money, the Ans were reunited with the three children they were forced to leave behind in Vietnam. When we were informed of the reunion, we saw it as a mairacle. The news media had pictures of Pastor An tearfully embracing his children, teenagers by that time.

The Dicht family is pastoring in California.

Our cultural exchange was a comedy of errors — and most of the errors were mine.

One day, though, Harold, upset about some political deal reported in the morning paper, pounded his fist on the breakfast table. The Vietnamese immediately went into a huddle! Often, when they didn't understand something, they went into a huddle. Poor Stan had to interpret all these huddles to us.

About the fist-banging, the Vietnamese concluded, "Jensens are in big fight!"

Poor Harold, he had to read the newspaper — and smile — whether he liked what he was reading or not!

Another huddle. And another interpretation. I had asked Harold to take out the garbage can on his way to the car.

"Poor Mr. Jensen, has to do woman's work," the pastors said. Harold loved it!

Finally, I said, "O.K., when I go to Vietnam, I'll do it Vietnam way. In America we *all* help! American tradition!"

That did it! Harold took out the garbage.

I'm a hugger—and made the mistake of hugging *everyone!* It took much interpretation for the men!

The priceless moments were when we read the Scriptures, prayed and sang together. The bond of Christian love transcends all barriers.

"I know He can use me—although sometimes I wonder why—to do His work."

The first Christmas together was a moving experience. My Norwegian mama gave a reading while Stan interpreted. Pastor An read the Christmas story in Vietnamese and they sang their carols. We did the same in English. God understands both.

Many changes have come since 1975. The Vietnamese joined with us when our brother Gordon was buried in the family plot on the Hammer homeplace beside my Norwegian papa. They understood. They had lived with death—but they also knew that "Jesus is the resurrection and the life." Someday we would all be together again.

They loved our Norwegian Mama because they have great respect for the wisdom that comes with age. And she understood their struggles. She told stories about coming to America herself and about learning English and adapting to new customs. There was no barrier in love. They heard her with their hearts.

At Christmastime in 1989, we received a beautiful letter from Hoi (Henry), the eldest son of Pastor An. He wrote:

> *I've been married for six months now and love every minute of it. I'm serving as a pastor of a Vietnamese Baptist Church in Tacoma, Washington. Besides that I am also attending the Golden Gate Baptist Theological Seminary on the Northwest Campus in Portland, Oregon.*

> *We have launched a new mission to sponsor refugees and to help them in the process of resettlement without neglecting the sharing of the gospel.*

In a previous letter he had told us about receiving his B.S. degree in Fairfax, Virginia, about going to the Philippines as a volunteer missionary, and about working in refugee camps there for two years.

He closed his Christmas letter, saying,

> *I've seen many of your books in the Northwest—so proud of you. Seems like yesterday we lived in Greensboro. All the sweet memories of our first settlement in the United States are fresh in my mind—plus the Four Seasons Mall, the school and the church. Please say hello to Dan, Ralph, and Chris, and the Lord richly bless you all.*

*I have never been too sure in my life that
this is what God wants me to do, and I know He
can use me—although sometimes I wonder why—
to do His work.*

> Love in Christ
> Henry Hoi Phan

As I tucked the letter back into the envelope, I thought back to that hot July day in 1975 when Hoi, swallowed up in a Navy pea coat, had come to us—shy, gaunt, hesitant.

We have our dreams and our plans. Sometimes they go awry, but God has His plan! His eternal purposes! For Hoi and his family, dreams in their homeland had crumbled but hope and dreams had risen again in a new country. God's promise had stood firm: "I will instruct thee and teach thee in the way which thou shalt go: I will guide thee with mine eye" (Psalm 32:8).

As I stowed Hoi's letter in the box marked KEEP, I began to chuckle. *Hoi,* I thought, *I'll still stick to my American tradition: no soy sauce on ice cream!*

GORDON HEDDERLY SMITH

He dreamed a dream,
And viewed from peak to peak,
Descended into valleys
Scanning higher heights to seek.

    He saw horizons
    Beyond the years of mortal man,
    Into time and space
    Of God's redemptive plan.

He spoke to mountains.
Trembling, they stepped aside
And bowed to unseen power
That would not be denied.

    The jungle groaned
    Beneath the awesome touch
    Of one who walked with God
    And gave so much.

The brush and tangled vine
Held the land in its hold,
Barring entrance with steaming breath
To this stranger bold.

    The grasses swayed,
    And monsoons wept with rain
    To close the entrance
    To this dark domain.

The ocean foamed
Against the sandy beach,
Defying anyone who roamed
Within her sheltered reach.

    But still He walked,
    Undaunted by the roar,
    Listening as God talked,
    Revealing something more.

The waves stood still,
And watched as God and man
Suffered the little one to come
According to God's eternal plan.

The years passed by;
The jungle brush gave way;
The tangled vines yielded—
For love had come to stay.

> The monsoons wept
> Upon the Sower's seed;
> The rain from Heaven fell,
> Pouring out for mankind's need.

Satan's kingdom trembled,
Lashed out with might unfurled,
Brought forth nations' armies—
War's destruction hurled.

> The jungle groaned;
> The monsoons wept with rain;
> The Crescent-China beach and ocean moaned
> With humanity in pain.

But here and there,
In mountains and tear-drenched earth,
Came forth eternal seed to bear
Redemption's plan—rebirth.

> His work was done.
> The waves and sea stood still.
> The mountains and the valleys heard
> His whisper, "Thy will be done."

The heavens opened.
As the gates swung open wide,
All the angels chorused,
"Earth, step aside."

> Let the music ring.
> And the glory unfold
> As the choirs sing
> Of God's grace—never old.

For Gordon has come,
Who moved a land by my Word.
Friend, I welcome you home,
You who honored me, your Lord.

—Margaret T. Jensen
February 1977

16

The Eighties

THE YELLOW RIBBONS were like banners waving *'round the old oak tree.*

Across the nation, tears of joy welcomed the release of Iranian hostages from the enemy camp. Hope rose high that the new decade of the eighties would usher in an era of peace and purpose.

A call for prayer sounded out over the lofty mountains, across the valleys, rivers and lakes, and into the cities and villages.

"Pray for America! We need a spiritual revival!" was like a theme song.

Know therefore that the LORD thy God, he is God, the faithful God which keepeth covenant and mercy with them that love him and keep his commandments to a thousand generations (Deuteronomy 7:9).

As long as the Israelites kept their part of the covenant, God blessed them. Would God lift His grace from America, as in the days of Israel, to allow drought, flood, pestilence, wars and persecution to turn His people back to Him?

How many years will the bells toll for the unborn generation? When will we weep for the children who were sacrificed to the gods of selfish pleasure as parents abandoned the traditional role of leadership?

America's voices sang with fervor, "God bless America." But when the blessings came, all too often, America's feet walked away to serve lesser gods.

As a nation, we wept when a child died from contaminated blood, but where was the cry of outrage that the blood was given by someone who defied God's laws to serve a god of lust?

We spent billions to find cures for diseases that could have been prevented by adhering to God's laws. We tore God's laws down from classroom walls and wondered why our children drifted out into a sea of permissive rebellion away from God and society.

Surely in the eighties America would return to the dream that had made America great — one nation, *under God*, with liberty and justice for all. Only then would we have a dream to give the rest of the world.

More than a century ago, men of God risked their lives, families and fortunes to battle against the evil of slavery. Today we need men of God to cry out from every church and synagogue in battle against the evil of slavery to the moral and spiritual decay that is destroying our civilization.

As we entered the eighties, we felt we surely had learned enough from the sixties and the seventies to turn America back to God. Surely we would see a great spiritual awakening where families and homes would be restored, and pulpits would once again resound with the authority of the prophets of God: "Thus saith the Lord!"

Would the decade of the eighties bring listening hearts? How would God speak to His people? Would we hear the still small voice of His Holy Spirit telling us to humble ourselves, to repent, to turn from our evil ways — and would God then heal our land?

May 18, 1980. The North Carolina spring came with gentle winds through the pampas grass. Azalea and dogwoods in pastel colors created a fairyland against a blue sky. I walked along the ocean shore where seagulls and sandpipers occupied the sandy beach. The tourists hadn't arrived yet, so the shore was quiet.

America was not alone in her suffering.

"I will lift up mine eyes to the hills." *Not too many hills here,* I mused, *only sand dunes.* The mighty rolling sea was a reminder of the old hymn, *Wonderful Grace of Jesus.*

World problems seemed to drift out to sea as I marveled at the wonders of God's creation.

Then I tuned in to the evening news.

Before us was the fury of Mount St. Helens like a monster breaking loose. It produced a twelve-mile-high column of smoke and ash. Six hundred thousand tons of ash fell on Yakima, Washington. A photographer was trapped in his car and suffocated in the volcanic ash.

Warnings had been sounded, but few people had heeded them!

The summer of 1980 began with tourists pouring into our area to enjoy the cool waves of Wrightsville Beach. It was sweltering weather.

The newspapers and TV reported a damaging heat wave across the nation. Before the heat wave ended in September, it had scorched states from Texas to the Dakotas, all the way up the East Coast to New England.

Janice and her family had never felt such discomfort. Like many New England homes, Janice's house had never needed air conditioning before.

The record temperatures killed crops, dried up reservoirs, felled livestock, buckled hundreds of miles of roads, burned out machinery, set off fires and turned buildings into ovens.

On the news we heard that property damage was estimated at $20 billion, and 1,265 lives had been claimed.

Then Hurricane Allen hit the mainland on September 9, 1980, and relief from the heat wave came to the Gulf Coast. Yet three lives were lost and the damages were $750 million.

America was not alone in her suffering. Somehow, all through the eighties, this gentle, peaceful world was gripped by fear as news poured in from other countries.

In December 1980, Italy was devastated by an earthquake. "Everything I ever worked for, for 30 years, is suddenly gone in 30 seconds," a survivor cried.

In March 1981, the headlines screamed, "Bitterman murdered!" Chet Bitterman, missionary, had been killed in Colombia, South America. Why?

Suddenly the eighties didn't seem so tranquil.

Hearts were failing for fear when Pan American Flight 759 fell from the sky on July 9, 1982. The last words they heard were: "You are sinking. Come on back!"

Eight crew members and 138 passengers were dead. Thirteen houses were leveled. In the wreckage of one house, a 16-month-old child was found alive.

When I read the words, "You are skinking. Come on back," I couldn't help but hear the prophets' warnings down through the centuries of time: "Return! Come on back! Remember how God led you! Return to your own truth! Don't worship false gods! Return to the old paths!"

Prayer groups across the land gathered and were praying, "Come back to God, America." What would it take to turn America back to God?

I read what John Adams wrote to his wife Abigail:

I am well aware of the toil and blood and treasure that it will cost us to maintain this Declaration and support and defend these States. Yet through the gloom I see rays of ravishing light and glory. I can see that the end is worth more than all the means.[1]

Today the battle is not all against a visible army with swords and guns. Much of it is against an invisible militant army, hostile to the Judeo-Christian heritage, the very values for which our fathers fought and died.

Surely America will once again stand tall, aware of the sacrifice to guard against the subtle erosion of the foundations of civilization.

On February 16, 1983, raging fires swept across Australia, devastating Victoria and South Australia.

Columbia's largest volcano rumbled to life and triggered a deadly tide of mud and melted snow. In the midst of the devastation, a Red Cross worker cradled a newborn baby.

In the midst of all of earth's upheaval, life somehow goes on. While some people eat, drink, and are merry, others pray for revival, and babies are born.

---

*Somehow my thoughts don't go to
the great moments in history, but to
the molten moments
within the fabric of our home.*

I hold in my hand the newspaper of January 29, 1986, and remember the terrible shock as we watched the Challenger space shuttle explode in flight, and its astronauts spiral to a fiery death.

On board was a beautiful school teacher, Christa McAuliffe.

President Reagan said, "We mourn seven heroes." It was the first in-flight disaster in fifty-six manned space missions. No one could ever forget the sight of that explosion against the blue sky. Prayers for the families swept across the world.

Only a few months later the world learned about the Chernobyl disaster. The blast spewed a cloud of radioactive gas around the world. In a country that doesn't believe in God, 70,000 people gathered for Mass in Kiev.

Many stories are told about a monster in Lake Nyos, Cameroun, West Africa. (Our grandsons enjoy the mystery stories that have been handed down from generation to generation.) Most of the herdsmen and farmers of this village were asleep in 1986 when suddenly more than 1700 people were dead.

An enormous invisible bubble of carbon monoxide was the monster that broke loose from the lake bottom sediment after being held in check for centuries. American experts thought that an earthquake had freed the Nyos monster from the lake bottom.

The natives had their own theories: either an angry chief had had his revenge or the spirit woman of the lakes and rivers had her revenge.

The tranquil blue lake became a lake of death.

We read in the Bible how men's hearts will fail them for fear in the last days. Were these catastrophes meant to be warnings to the world as to how frail man is when compared to the awesome power of God's creation?

The Bible says, *Fear Not!* How can we not fear? The Bible reminds us to number our days and tells us that we are as frail as the grass. The Bible also says that when we see these things—wars, rumors of wars, earthquakes, famines—then we are to lift up our heads, not to cower in fear, but to remember that the light and the glory is ahead. God has made us for eternity and one day this old world will all pass away.

We must take the opportunity to teach our children that only God, His Throne, His Word, and His children are forever settled.

In this world the mountains will erupt, the sea will rage, the winds will blow, fires and drought will come. The only place of safety is in the hollow of God's hand.

I could almost hear my sister, Joyce, singing, "We have this moment to hold in our hand." Somehow my thoughts don't go to the great moments in history, but to the molten moments within the fabric of our home—a first step, a kiss for a cut finger, building a castle in the sand, walking along the sea, the family laughing and talking around the table, a child's prayer; unselfish love for each other.

God's hand reaches us, even in the disasters of life, and draws us to Himself—and home!

Our grandsons fill us in on news from the sports world and are quick to point out the strong Christian witness from coaches and players. When drugs destroy a hero, they are devastated. They take it as a personal blow.

"How can they do this, Gram?" one grandson asked. "Even my friends at school don't seem to care what drugs can do. I even went to a high school party and there was nothing to drink except beer; not even a coke or gingerale. Besides, it was illegal. All of us were under age. I just left and came home—disgusted!"

At Christmas time Shawn, 17, invited all the basketball team for Christmas dinner. Ralph and the boys had been hunting. Chris, an expert in preparation of venison, prepared a feast that included her specialty, pecan and custard pies.

The team decided that this should be an annual event! I'm inclined to agree.

Around our table we often spoke of what was happening in the world. We spoke of man's prediction about the coming of the Lord and the false doctrine of setting dates!

We also spoke of the signs and prophecies that are being fulfilled before our eyes — and ignored by many.

It is not our responsibility to set dates, we agreed, but to be ready and occupy until Jesus comes. Somehow it seemed that the warnings were coming every time we turned on the news.

We spoke of how the world watched and prayed for two and a half days when two-year-old Jessica McClure from Midland, Texas, fell into an abandoned well. Rescuers had to drill through hard rock to rescue her. No effort was too great! On October 16, 1987, the world rejoiced as that little girl was taken from the well. Yet during that time hundreds of babies were taken from what should have been the safest "well" of all — to die, not to live. A cheer went up from the world when Jessica was safe. Who mourned for the unborn?

When I was speaking in Toronto, we heard about the Armenian earthquake. Relief supplies were sent from around the world.

I cut out one picture from the paper: a beautiful dark-eyed four-year-old girl holding her doll.

The mother and daughter were trapped for eight days, unable to move under the debris. The child cried from thirst. The mother reached around and found a piece of glass and cut her finger so the child could suck the blood. "I knew I was going to die, but I wanted my daughter to live," she said.

They were both rescued.

Another story was told of how a father who held his infant daughter in his hands outside a window. The father died, but the child lived.

And I hear in my heart the song:

> On a hill far away
> Stood an old rugged cross.

Yes, Someone died for me, too.

In June of 1989, there was a picture on the news media of a lone woman facing the tanks of China. This young woman walked fearlessly toward the invading soldiers in Tiananmen Square to tell them they were not welcome in her city. The soldiers fired! She fell!

The massacre of hundreds of people blackened the name of an army once famed for bravery.

"The army comes from the people," one man cried. "How can they kill their own?"

We have since been told how out of the depth of China's suffering thousands in that country have turned to God, to find meaning in life. Jesus is the way, the truth and the life. No man comes to the Father but by Him.

We watched the news in horror and prayed for the brave youth of China.

In Wilmington, by the sea, we toured the great mercy ship, Anastasis. When the ship docked, members of several churches, including ours, Myrtle Grove Presbyterian Church, served as hosts, taking the crew shopping and providing meals.

While death and destruction waged war across the world in China, this one mercy ship prepared to take medical and humanitarian relief as well as spiritual help to third world countries.

God always has His band of Gideons, small in number, but serving a great God.

Again man's inhumanity to man made headlines — terrorists holding hostages, a plane filled with young people, crashed — a suspected terrorist bomb. Innocent people suffer!

I picked up a *Life* magazine and read the front cover: "Finding God on Flight 232".[2] A United DC10 enroute from Denver to Chicago had to make an emergency landing in Sioux City, Iowa. While landing, the engine tipped and the plane's wing struck the ground.

One survivor said, "I was sitting on the edge of eternity."

Another one said, "I think I went through this for a purpose — to show that God can still be seen and felt and glorified in the face of tragedy."

A third person said, "A second chance has been given to me."

Are we teaching our children that, even in the face of sitting on the edge of eternity, it is not the end, ONLY THE BEGINNING? God's hand reaches us, even in the disasters of life, and draws us to Himself — and home!

I was speaking in Wisconsin on September 21, 1989, when I heard the news about Hurricane Hugo. When I returned home I was thankful that Wilmington had been spared, but Charleston, South Carolina, and Charlotte, North Carolina, were in the direct path of both the hurricane and tornadoes.

Our friend, Mary, loaded up her car with jugs of drinking water, chests of ice, clothing, blankets and food to take to her relatives in Charleston. Relief came from everywhere—states, churches and individuals who headed to the stricken areas to rebuild not only broken buildings but broken dreams.

Franklin Graham, president of The Samaritan's Purse, headed a caravan of mobile homes to bring housing to a stricken black community.

An abbot from a Catholic monastery said, "Circumstances do not make us; they reveal us."

When my Charlotte friend, Muriel Sandbo, returned to her house, she found her beautiful home badly damaged and the stately trees tumbled like matchsticks. "The emotional shock is greater than the physical," she said, "For suddenly you know nothing is permanent."

I could almost hear Mama singing years before in the second floor flat in Chicago,

> "This world is not my home,
> I'm just a-passing through."

Now she was really home—and safe!

Hugo cost North Carolina farmers $165 million. Dairy farmers dumped $150,000 worth of milk because of no refrigeration. Unmilked cows became sick. Loss of timber reached more than $62 million in losses. Apple and peach trees were pulled out by the roots.

Just a few weeks later, in California, at 5:04 P.M., October 17, 1989, an earthquake stopped clocks and shook Candlestick Park where thousands were awaiting the start of the third game of the world series between the Oakland Athletics and the San Francisco Giants.

The evacuation of the park was orderly and free from panic. Yet on our TV screen it was like watching a disaster movie—the collapse of the Bay Bridge Freeway, a car disappearing into a gaping hole, people being trapped in cars and crushed when Cyprus Street Viaduct of the Nimitz Freeway fell apart, the fires and destruction that followed.

Once again Americans reached out to rebuild broken homes and broken dreams.

Tragedy and comedy, agony and ecstasy—all a part of life.

I recall writing down a strange dream I had one night. Most of my dreams aren't worth mentioning, let alone writing them down. I'm usually singing a solo in my nightgown or finding myself in church with mismatched shoes—or worse!

This dream was worth remembering. I saw Jesus filling a large gold bowl with all-colored leaves, some bright colors and some dark.

"What are you doing?" I asked in my dream.

Jesus smiled. "Oh, I'm just working the all things together for good."

Even the decade of the eighties? I wondered.

1. Peter Marshall, *The Light and the Glory* (Old Tappan, NJ: Fleming H. Revell Company, 1940), in the Introduction, on the passing of the Declaration of Independence.

2. *Life* magazine, September 1989.

17

Life Goes On

THOUGH THE DECADE of the eighties heralded one natural disaster after the other, in between those events, life still went on.

For example, in the midst of the 1989 Hugo disaster, we had a "believe-it-or-not" wedding in Myrtle Grove Church.

The groom, on his way to the wedding, was in the plane that slid into New York's East River. He was fished out of the sea. On the day of the wedding, Hugo threatened to slam Wilmington, but turned to Charleston and then turned, at 45 miles an hour, toward Charlotte.

The ring was lost. The plans for a Virgin Islands honeymoon had to be canceled due to the hurricane and looting. Even the limousine would be late to take the bride and groom to the reception at the Surf Club.

It rained all morning, but rays of sunshine filled the church by 6 P.M.

"This is a special occasion in ordinary circumstances, but it is a great occasion today," said Pastor Horace Hilton. He turned to the groom and continued, "I honestly believe God spared your life. This wedding was intended to be, Mr. and Mrs. Thomas Newberry."

What a story to tell their children!

As a family we entered the eighties in Wilmington. We had moved there in 1978. Day-by-day duties demanded our attention, but in that decade I began to write—at first to recall memories for our children. *First We Have Coffee* was published in 1982.

The *Lena* book followed as a message of hope and encouragement to parents who are grieving over wayward children. In 1984 I began to travel and the airplane became my second home.

In different parts of the country God has given me special families who adopt me as an "extra grandma." Besides these, He has given me hundreds of precious friends.

Dr. Eldred Nelson and his wife Ruth were the first family to "take me in" when I trekked across the country from North Carolina to Seattle, Washington, for the first time. Each year we enjoy a "family reunion" with the Nelsons and the Inez Glass family in Gig Harbor. There's a need for open hearts and homes across the country to welcome weary travelers.

As I shared the stories of faith and humor from my childhood, I watched people whose lives had been shattered by the storms of life, bowed down by unbearable sorrow, bitter and brittle over cruel wrongs. They listened, received, and yielded to God's Spirit.

Often I held them in my arms and prayed for God to keep them in His care.

In between my travels, I kept writing and speaking. TV and radio talk shows and community projects became other areas of communicating God's unconditional love.

In looking through one of my file "boxes" recently (I never seem to get them all emptied), I found a copy of a letter I wrote to my four sisters in June of 1987.

It was BARGAIN WEEK with Margaret Jensen.

Dear Grace, Doris, Joyce and Jeanelle,

I'm sitting on the runway — waiting for take-off to go back home to Wilmington.

Last Saturday when I arrived in Chicago, Jim Warren, host for Prime Time America, met me, and I ate lunch with his lovely wife Jean.

Sunday A.M. Jim picked me up and we went to the Willow Creek Community Church where 9,000 people attend the two Sunday morning services. Streams of traffic flowed like a river while policemen directed the oncoming cars, an incredible sight. Literally thousands of young people packed the beautiful building that was surrounded by trees and lakes with ducks swimming in formation.

The music is sometimes contemporary, and the young pastor, a walking dynamo, gave a sermon on the subject of "Amazing Grace."

Dwight Ellefsen and his family picked me up after church and we proceeded to Rockford to the golden wedding anniversary of Gladys and Tom Ellefsen. Gladys, a nursing classmate of mine, was beautiful in a deep aqua and lace gown — lovely! Two bridesmaids made the celebration — and I was one of them.

Monday I began a most fascinating challenge, an unforgettable experience. As we drove through the city, the skyscrapers towered above us. All around humanity streamed in all directions. Then we came to tall red brick buildings — a serene monument to a man of God and his dream — The Moody Bible Institute!

To think, Grace, that when you and I attended evening classes at Moody, it cost only a nickel for carfare and a nickel for a bowl of soup! We were so rich, and now we realize it more than ever.

I was taken to the offices on the tenth floor and introduced to the staff of Prime Time America. News reports came thick and fast, and I was suddenly a part of a world of communication that moves a hundred miles an hour.

Telephone calls to Boston, California, Atlanta — separating truth from rumors — also receiving an input of wisdom from great men. All this I was a part of (via phone) and I stand in awe of the behind-the-scenes work (16 hours a day). For Jim, it doesn't stop even then.

I also saw what it was like to scuttle about for one show. A half-hour before air time, secretaries, producers, host and even me, the co-host, scurried to the eighth floor studio, gathered books, notes, pens and a glass of ice water. Then we stopped for prayer. The lights flashed on and it was count-down!

"Good afternoon. This is Jim Warren of Prime Time America and, to my co-host, Margaret Jensen, welcome to Chicago!" The music came on, then news reports, and live interviews from Europe, Canada and California. And I was on!

My mind went back to the 5-cent soup and the 5-cent streetcar fare—and now, here I was! The two and a half hours seemed to fly.

It was BARGAIN WEEK with Margaret Jensen. (Incidentally, I worked this out on the plane, and Jim okayed it.)

The window on my side was shattered into a million pieces (back seat also) and someone snatched my purse!

Monday, *The Bargain of Giving*. I used stories, of course, and last of all my punch line: I gave my life to Jesus at 6 years of age. God got only me but I got God—a real bargain!!

We had been through a very hard day. We had to deal with heartbreaking news from around the world, but we also heard accounts of God's faithful people sharing their love and faith with a suffering humanity.

The staff picked up papers and locked the studio. What a studio—so incredibly beautiful—with a wooden carving that says, "Let the words of my mouth be acceptable." They have the most modern equipment, and such talent! Jim is one of the most creative people I've met—music, art, drama, and a voice and presence that moves people to action. I stand in awe that I could even be on his program—also in awe of the guests who appear on P.T.A. in person and by phone.

My first day came to a close and Jim and I were on the way to supper in his home where Jean was waiting.

We were in the Austin area, stopped at a red light. Traffic was heavy at 6:30 P.M. Suddenly we heard a *boom*. The window on my side was shattered into a million pieces (back seat also) and someone snatched my purse. They call it "smash and grab." It took two seconds. Jim saw two teens running through the alley, so he jumped out of the car and took off after them. But then he yielded to wisdom and we took off to the police. It was so routine to the police—forms, questions, etc. There was no chance of recovery. My airplane ticket home, $125 in cash, all my identification, my glasses and my keys—all were gone!

Just that quickly it came to me: "In everything give thanks." We were not hurt, even by the shards of glass. We had a sense of God's protection as we headed home to Jean and and their son Randy and a wonderful supper; then back to other friends in River Forest to stay overnight. A quick call and Harold put everything in motion to arrange a new return plane ticket.

In the morning my new friend had a lovely purse, ready for me. In it were a lipstick and a comb along with a change purse containing $25. How grateful I was—a woman without a purse and lipstick is really lost!

Tuesday—a new program for the new day. The theme was *The Bargain of Yielding*—I spoke of yielding the right-of-way at a red light, yielding to wisdom (a warning to hide purses and not to get out of the car), and yielding to God's will.

We did more. Jim called an inner-city preacher who gave a run-down of the work at his location, including a new gym, a health clinic, legal advice, and counsel for youth and church.

We used this story to make people aware of the needs in the inner city. We asked for ball teams and church groups to supply balls, bats and basketballs for the gym. We also prayed for the two boys who had robbed me. I know God will turn it all for good.

While sirens cry into the night and the traffic jams pile up all day because of the people-to-people shuffle, the voice of WMBI reaches around the world.

Wednesday I talked about *The Bargain of Obedience*. Obedience *is* a bargain. Jean and Randy picked me up after the broadcast and we went back to the Willow Creek Church in the evening. It was packed with 4000-5000 people, and most were young people. A dynamic message, electric music, praise choruses, and then a communion service.

Thursday was *The Bargain of Forgiveness*. God forgives us — what a bargain! This was another busy day filled with interviews with authors, executives and missionaries.

Friday was the *Bargain of Love*. Nothing separates us from the love of God. Again, what a bargain!

Love,
Margaret

If you ask me, a life given to God is the very best bargain of any that we can make!

18

Twisted by Storms

IT WAS A BEAUTIFUL Sunday afternoon and I was back home with my family. While Chris and Harold watched the girls build castles in the sand and kept a sharp eye on the boys as they chased each other over the dunes, my sturdy, six-foot-six son and I walked along the beach. "Mother," Ralph said, "you won't believe who came to see me when you were speaking in California."

"Oh, no. What did I miss this time?"

"Well, I'll tell you what you missed. You missed meeting Ed! You'll never believe what he has been doing! Remember him?"

Ed? Oh, yes. I remembered Ed.

My mind went back to the night in Wenham, Massachusetts, chronicled in the chapter "The Winds of Winter" in my book *Lena*. I remembered that night as if I had been there myself.

The reflection of the moonlight had laid a shimmering gleam across the frozen lake. A chilled wintry wind cut its biting path down from Canada through the barren trees on the Gordon College campus.

The college kids were dressed for the New England winter—knit scarves wrapped around their necks, fleece-lined jackets buttoned to the chin, toboggan caps pulled down over their ears, their fingers curled in woolly mittens. Still the feeling of frostbite nipped at their faces.

Rob noticed a solitary skater
cutting across the lake,
dangerously near the zone
where the hidden springs kept the ice thin.

Laughter filled the air as they built a bonfire on the solid part of the ice, far from the danger zone where hidden springs kept part of the lake from freezing completely. The fire crackled and snapped. Happy sounds rose from carefree students gliding in rhythmic patterns over the ice.

Four boys slipped away from the crowd, cutting a defiant path as they raced across the lake with a forbidden bottle of brandy. In the darkness—not missed by the others—they downed their brandy and felt its warmth burning their throats and stomachs.

Ralph, our tall lean southern boy—the son who loved cornbread and grits and cherry pie—was one of them. He had left home for college, carving out a growing pattern of rebellion, his heart bent on doing things his own way, his once mischievous blue eyes sullen and moody now.

His friends, Rob, Ed and David—their faces barely discernible in the shadows—huddled in the darkness with him. As one of the boys tipped the brandy bottle, Rob noticed a solitary skater cutting across the lake, dangerously near the zone where the hidden springs kept the ice thin.

Before he could shout a warning, the cracking ice and a piercing cry broke the stillness as Allen, Ralph's big college brother, disappeared from sight.

Rob was off at once, the other three right behind him. Unexpectedly, Rob plunged into the inky blackness too, the numbness of the brandy gone as he slipped into the icy water.

"I'll get Rob," Ralph called out to Ed. "You two go get Allen."

Even as Ralph helped Rob struggle back to safety, Ed dropped into the black gaping hole in a desperate effort to rescue Al. "Make a chain," he begged.

The four, their teeth chattering, formed a human chain and almost succeeded in dragging Allen to the surface as other skaters raced toward them. But the fast-moving current snatched him from their grip and his heavy skates and wet, frozen clothing dragged him beneath the ice floe into eternity.

For several moments it looked as though Ed would go deep into the freezing water as well, but the others screamed for him to hang on. Time stood still as they gradually pulled him to the safety of the solid ice.

Numb from cold and shock—tears frozen on their cheeks—the four brushed past the rest of the students and made their way from the bitter wintry wonderland back to the empty solace of the dormitory. Standing in a warm shower, they were able to get out of their frozen clothing as it thawed, but nothing could remove the cold grip of despair that held them.

Later, as they knelt in the chapel, guilt overwhelmed them. "My God, we tried," one of them cried in anguish.

The others took up his prayer. "If we hadn't been at that end of the lake, no one would even have seen Allen."

"Oh, God, we tried. We tried . . . "

They couldn't get away from the fact that Allen was on the threshold of life. He was to graduate from college in just a few weeks and begin his life's work. Instead, he had begun his journey in eternity.

The thought of eternity offered them no comfort until Ralph cut the black despair that engulfed them with "We've got to remember, Allen was a Christian. He's really not dead but home with the Lord. He was a believer." Then he added, "What if it had been us?"

"Yeah, Ralph. What if it had been us?"

The question dangled in the air.

At 2 A.M. word reached the four rebels: Divers had found Allen's body downstream. Despair engulfed them afresh. At the memorial service, hope filtered through their rebellion again — but only briefly.

Ralph slouched in the pew as the preacher proclaimed, "I am the resurrection and the life; he that believeth in Me . . . shall never die."

Allen's mother, crushing Ed to her, said, "You boys risked your lives to save my son."

Her love cushioned their deep pain but the winter of their souls — the darkness of their own sin — would keep its hold on these four rebels for a much longer time.

Back in Greensboro, I wondered why there was no mail from my son. It was the silence of a dark winter night in my own soul as well.

* * *

Yes, I clearly remembered Ed that Sunday afternoon as Ralph and I walked the beach. For a few moments, we walked quietly. Ralph would never forget.

His witness for Jesus was so bold that he was put into prison in a foreign land. He thought it was the end for him.

I had wondered what happened to Ed, the one who plunged into the icy hole. He always had been fun to be with, daring and radical. Then came that night when Al slipped from their grasp. What was Ed like now?

"You know, Mom," Ralph said at last, "we were all twisted by storms, but God polished us with His love. It is like the wood I work with, such shades of color, twisted by storms and made beautiful by God's hand."

I waited. "What did happen to Ed?" I asked finally.

"It's a miracle, Mom, a miracle. Ed became a missionary. His witness for Jesus was so bold that he was put in prison in a foreign land. He thought it was the end for him, and there he sat, in his dark dungeon. Then one day someone appeared at his cell, opened the door, and said, 'You are free to go, but you must leave the country.' Ed never knew how it happened — but thank God for the miracle that got him released."

Just think — Ed, a missionary! That fun-loving, challenging character, always ready for a dare, now has a divine mission — witnessing to the grace of God.

"Mom, I only hope he can come back someday so you can meet him. Do you realize how, one by one, we've all returned to the sea to show what God has done? Remember how we were so sure it had to be the farm to bring them home? The farm had its purpose in the beginning — we all loved the rugged land — but it was just for a season."

"We are also called to tell our stories by the sea, Ralph."

He nodded. "Dad was right! He was so sure it was God's will for us to move to Wilmington. Mom, you may never have written the books if you hadn't come here — away from all the activity you were involved with."

"Talking about books, you won't believe what happened to me. While autographing books in a bookstore, a handsome young man in suit coat and tie, with his beautiful wife, looked at me and said, 'Hi, Mom. You don't recognize me, do you? I know, I have a tie on!'"

"I looked. 'Oh, Jim!' We hugged and laughed together. The last time I saw Jim he was long-haired and barefoot — no tie, not even a shirt. Today he is a minister in North Carolina."

We had linked arms now — my son and I.

"Oh, Ralph, I can see them coming, one by one, then with their families: Kevin (wouldn't Keith have loved the ocean?), Rob, Jack, Jim, Tommy, Doug—and now Ed. I'm sure more will come—perhaps have a reunion. Each one with a story to tell, a story of God's faithfulness to all generations. Their children will hear the stories by the sea and in years to come will tell them in their own way."

It was evening time, when boats turn toward the harbor, children gather sandbuckets and sea gulls sit in a row and watch the fading of another day. White clouds against the blue sky turn a soft pink and the waves catch the lingering rays of the sun.

It was time to go home to toasted cheese sandwiches, potato chips, lemonade and cookies—standard Sunday night fare. A day is never wasted when it holds a memory, and our day held many memories.

It was late into the night when I thought again of Allen whose icy hand had slipped from Ed's grasp—only to have God reach down with His mighty hand and take him home—safe evermore.

> From sinking sand He lifted me.
> With tender Hand He lifted me.

Yes, "my boys" have a story to tell—and they are telling it.

19

The Storm

WRIGHTSVILLE BEACH

Unending, grasping sea,
Forever reaching for the shore;
Is the sky not enough for you?
Yet, you reach for more.

    Never ending, gently lapping
    Billows, angry with the spray,
    Reaching, grasping at the sand
    While night follows day.

Sometimes laughing in the sun,
Then angry, with billowing foam
Breaking high to splash the clouds,
Then rolling back home.

    Restless, rollicking, ruthless, rolling,
    Tempting, tempestuous, tossing, turning,
    Splashing with sunlight, crying with rain,
    Playful or angry—always churning.

Sometimes I hate you, love you, fear you—
Held captive by your power;
Cold salt spray, relentless hold,
A willing prisoner by the hour.

THE COLD WIND of October 1988 encouraged me to button up my jacket and tighten the scarf around my head. The beach was deserted again. Tourists had long ago picked up their umbrellas and blankets and closed their beach houses for the winter. College students were catching up from a long playful summer.

I carried my familiar bag of bread and out of nowhere the sea gulls came dipping and soaring to fight over the scraps. When the bread was gone, they were gone, too, to faraway places.

There is something about the sea that calls us back again and again. When a storm comes up, so do traffic jams, just so the people in the cars can get to the shore to see how high the waves are. Police firmly, continually, redirect traffic back into town.

Today the sea was peaceful and the sky was blue, but the wind reminded me that summer was over and winter was coming. I walked around the bend to the Coast Guard station, found a stump, and just sat.

Someone once asked an old woman, gnarled from farm work and sun, what she was doing in that rocking chair on her weather-beaten porch. "Well, I reckon I just sits . . . and rocks . . . and thinks, and then again . . . sometimes I just sits," she said.

So I just sat! It was difficult to believe that this peaceful ocean, with its playful waves, could one day have brought near disaster to us. Besides just "sitting," I also allowed my thoughts to go back to that day of near disaster.

It was a Tuesday morning in September 1984. Television and radio stations canceled regular programs to keep the public informed about the unpredictable hurricane Diana which was blowing off the coast of North

Carolina. It was the most massive and threatening hurricane since Hazel in 1954.

I remembered a story from Hazel about an old man who had lost everything. Searching through the debris of his home, the man was surprised to find his fishing pole. He picked it up and headed for the now quiet beach.

"Where in the world are you going?" his distraught wife cried.

"Can't think of no better time to fish," the man answered, "and sort out my head." (Our fishermen love that story.)

At her appointed time, the leading lady turned to churn and roar her way toward shore.

Ralph and his family came to our house to wait out Diana with us.

The monstrous, angry waves of the storm roared, and reached for man-made dunes, cupping up mounds of beachfront with giant fingers. The winds came in a fury, and the rain hammered our boarded-up windows.

We filled the bathtub with water and kept large kettles filled with drinking water. Long lines had waited in grocery stores to stock up on food supplies, flashlights and batteries.

Before the power went off, Chris and I prepared a large kettle of soup, some coffee and lots of cookies—emergency fare.

At 3 A.M. Wednesday, the ill-humored Diana was lashing to be free, yet held at bay forty miles off shore. At her appointed time, the leading lady turned to churn and roar her way toward shore. High tides and torrential rain continued.

On Thursday at 3 A.M., the winds struck the coast at 125 miles per hour; the pounding surf leveled the sand dunes and knocked out power lines.

The roar of the wind drowned our voices. We kept praying until sparks of faith rekindled the flame in our fearful hearts.

Tornado warnings followed. We all wrapped ourselves in blankets and huddled on the screened-in porch and prayed. Trees swayed like grasses.

Back inside the house, we read Psalm 91 by candlelight:

Thou shalt not be afraid for the terror by night (verse 5, KJV).

Yet we shivered in our fear! Ralph's furniture showroom could be wiped out by the Cape Fear River rolling down Market Street. The factory with its expensive machinery and priceless woods and partially finished furniture lay in the path of the tornado. It could all be destroyed and priceless antiques wiped out!

We huddled together, and we read Psalm 93:1:

The LORD reigneth, he is clothed with majesty . . .

The wind screamed through the pine trees. It sounded like a freight train. The trees bent to the ground.

Thy throne is established of old: thou art from everlast-
ing (Psalm 93:2).

We cried out together, "Oh, Lord, our trust is in
You. Stay the power of nature's fury. You alone ride upon
the wings of the wind."

The roar of the wind drowned our voices. We kept
praying until sparks of faith rekindled the flame in our
fearful hearts.

I will say of the LORD, He is my refuge and my fortress:
my God; in him will I trust (Psalm 91:2).

The morning came, and the rain turned gentle.
The trees shook off the terror of the night and stood tall
again. Neighbors came with hot coffee prepared on kero-
sene camping stoves.

The sun came out to bring courage and warmth to
a new day. With fear and trembling, Harold and Ralph
headed off in the truck to view the damage at the shop.
Wonder of wonders, the showroom was dry! The river had
raged outside the door, but it had not entered.

Across the road to the sound, trees had snapped in
the path of the tornado. Ralph eased the truck around the
debris, and got to the factory. All around the factory the
trees had fallen, but *away from the building!* There was
no damage!

O sing unto the LORD a new song; for He hath done
marvelous things (Psalm 98:1).

Across the ocean front, the sand walls had just
crumbled. Deep within our family the walls of faith had
grown stronger.

The memories wouldn't stop, but it was time now
for me to go home. The sun cast a glow over the peaceful

ocean, and fishing boats were returning to the shore, sea gulls following close behind.

The storm seemed so long ago; yet remembering, I realized afresh how fragile life is. "We have this moment to hold in our hands." I left the isolated stump on the beach and went to my car and drove home. Once there, I eased the car into its place, brushed off the sand, and put on the coffeepot.

Late into the night, I continued to ponder the storms of life.

THE STORM OF THE SOUL

I saw the storm — black, threatening clouds.
Salt spray with stinging sand
Beat at my heart and whipped my faith.
I covered my fears with my hand.

Doubts thundered with deafening noise,
So I ran from the threatening storm.
Stumbling and falling, I heard a voice:
"Turn in to the storm — to Me."

My eyes were blinded by salt and tears;
My faith slipped in the sand.
My heart was beating with unknown fears,
But I turned to the storm — and His Hand.

Over the noise of the angry storm,
I heard Him call my name.
"You are hidden with me — safe in My care
From eternity to eternity — I am the same."

20

The Choice

ONE EVENING IN the summer of 1985, a year after Hurricane Diana, I hurried across the grass of the campus to join the thousands gathering for the Youth Crusade held in the Task Coliseum of the University of North Carolina in Wilmington.

I made my way around hundreds of young people sitting on the floor and found a seat high in the bleachers. From there, I watched the auditorium fill with people from various denominational and cultural backgrounds.

Barefooted young people mingled with impeccably groomed sophisticates. Music and preaching filled the air with a joyful sound — a sound of faith in an unbelieving world, hope in a despairing world, and love in a world of hate.

When the invitation was extended to accept Jesus, the only way, the truth, and the life, young and old moved together toward the counseling area. Prominent businessmen and respected professional men walked with the flow of humanity to extend their help in prayer in counseling.

Beside me in the bleachers, a young man pleaded with his friend to accept Christ as his personal Savior. The friend resisted, but his face wore an expression of deep misery.

I reached over and took his hand. "God loves you, and we want to help you," I told him.

Tears filled his eyes. He seemed to waver. Then, with a determined, "I'll do it," he ran down the bleachers toward the counseling room. A prominent lawyer put his arm around him and together they walked into the room.

---

*The young man stood there — a picture
of agony and despair. I went to him
and gathered him into my arms
and said, "Oh, God loves you.*

Across the aisle I watched a young girl plead with a young couple to accept Christ. The girlfriend wept, and turned to her boyfriend and asked him to go with her. He shook his head with a determined "no" and the girl left with her friend. With a backward glance, she beckoned her boyfriend to follow. He shook his head. She went on alone, sobbing.

The young man stood there — a picture of agony and despair. I went to him and gathered him into my arms and said, "Oh, God loves you; come, meet our son and let him tell you his story."

When the service ended, Ralph was still telling the young man the story of his conversion from drugs to God's gift of salvation. The young man wept.

When his girlfriend returned, she found him weeping his way to the foot of the cross where God makes all things new. They wept tears of joy in each other's arms.

It was late when our car pulled slowly into the night traffic, but some new Christians joined our family around the table for grilled cheese sandwiches and lemonade, and the stories continued.

One young man had listened to a tape from a friend's Sunday school class. It was about Ralph's conversion. The young man pulled over to the side of the road to ask Jesus into his life. Then he came to the crusade to pray for his family, and he left determined to share his faith with them and with his friends.

I listened to prominent businessmen tell how their priorities had been rearranged.

A lonely tourist from Canada wandered into the Coliseum out of curiosity. He left with a purpose in life.

Two teenage boys with a drug problem came to the crusade with friends and came forward to ask for prayer and help. Later, the boys' parents, steeped in the traditions of "another faith," refused to allow the boys to receive follow-up help from the minister who had counseled them at the crusade. The parents could not accept what had happened to their sons, and the enemy was enabled to snatch the seed of faith away from the boys. Now the parents weep over their wayward sons.

During the service in my home church on the Wednesday night following the crusade, I listened to prominent businessmen tell how their priorities had been rearranged. The Bible study was set aside as the spontaneous stories continued.

Another local pastor recalled how he had received a call from a woman in a neighboring town. She requested prayer for her brother who was a prominent businessman in Wilmington and was adamant against gospel meetings. Each month the pastor placed the man's name on the calendar for prayer.

During the crusade a counselor gave this pastor the name of a man who had just received Christ as his Savior. With a cry of joy, the pastor recognized the name of the man from Wilmington. *The effectual, fervent prayer of a righteous man availeth much,* I thought.

A former bar owner, under deep conviction, was encouraged to attend the crusade, and there he had an encounter with the one who can make all things new. As a result, two bars were sold, and the man's wife and daughter were born again. Later, his mother was brought to a local church and also was born again.

The fruit continued as this new Christian family brought another friend. When that friend was converted, he in turn brought his family to Christ.

The crusade passed, but the choices remain.

After the crusade, I walked across the campus again one early morning, and I recalled the message that rang out hope for despair, joy for sorrow and love for hate. It told of a new beginning for all of mankind in Christ Jesus. Our choices affect everyone around us. Only eternity will reveal the results of the choices made during that crusade.

One outstanding choice was related by a local pastor. He told a story about ducks swimming in fenced-in ponds, quacking at each other through the fences. One day a heavy rain came, filling the ponds until they covered the fences over. The ducks then decided to swim together as one.

The choice, the decision made by the Christian leaders of Wilmington to blend doctrinal diversities into one effort to reach humanity with the message of "so great salvation," made all the other choices possible — "That they may be one" (John 17).

Sometimes fences must be taken down — or perhaps flooded over — for us to get together in Christian unity.

21

The Edge of Eternity

Thanksgiving 1989, and the family was gathered around the festive table. Sarah loved these family gatherings. "Papa," she said to Harold, "I love it—everybody crowded around the table and talking at the same time—nobody listening. I love it!"

The hard part was when the table was too crowded, and the two youngest girls had to sit in the breakfast room. But today we solved it—we brought in a sturdy TV tray and seated the girls close to us. "We just don't want to miss anything, Grammy," Sarah said.

Somehow the conversation shifted to the decade that was closing and began to focus on what the decade of the nineties would usher in.

Some scientists predicted greater natural disasters. Theologians spoke of prophecies being fulfilled that could usher in the coming of our Lord Jesus Christ.

How then do we live?

Jesus said, "Occupy, until I come."

The children recounted the disasters of the eighties. They also knew that even if life on this earth ended, life was only beginning. We are made for eternity.

"By the way, Ralph," I said, "I talked to Kevin and they are all fine. They're talking about going back to Mexico. Susan may have to regain her health in the States, but their hearts are with their people."

The conversation shifted from crumbling walls and earthquakes to crumbling political and religious powers. And then we talked about what had stood. What did not crumble!

"Mom, do you realize we are all standing? Chris and I came through the turbulence of the sixties and saw God's power in the seventies. Now our children are meeting my old friends—the very ones society gave up on—but God's love made them all new—including me."

Ralph leaned back in his chair and went on, "Look at Rob, working with troubled youth—he was once so bitter, and now look how he loves the Lord. He didn't crumble."

"Oh yes," Chris said, "and I talked with Peggy and Tom Smith from Greensboro. They told me that Jack and Adrian will return to their mission work in Mexico as soon as their daughter is settled in college." Chris cut the pies—her own specialties, pecan and coconut— while she filled us in on the news.

"That's not all, Ralph," I chimed in. "A woman called me who read the *Lena* book and said, 'Jim is our new pastor, and he promised to bring me to Wilmington to meet you.' "

A recent letter from Billy's mother had filled us in on his teaching in a Bible school. This is the rascal who climbed in my windows—just for fun. Ralph and Billy had been friends from second grade and shared all their mischievous activities through the years.

"Why don't you knock and come in through the door, Billy?" I asked one day.

"Windows are more fun," he grinned.

One day he opened the window of his heart, and God climbed in.

One by one, in faraway places, "my boys" are standing. Walls around the world may crumble, but the child of God is forever.

I swallowed hard and poured out my own heart. "Just look at what God has allowed us to see."

Harold's gaze met mine. "I know it was difficult to make changes, Margaret, but I have never been so sure of anything as that the move to Wilmington was of God." Harold paused. "I prayed and asked God for guidance, and now that we have gone through these turbulent eighties, we can see how God led us all, step by step.

"Everything else can crumble around us: plans, dreams, hopes—we can experience even great losses—but the child of God is eternal, kept by His power. Forever, God's Word is settled in heaven, and God's throne is from eternity to eternity."

Harold glanced around the table, his gaze settling briefly on each face. His son. His daughter. His grandchildren. "I want you children to remember that when disasters strike, you are in God's hand. If your Grammy or Papa should be taken home, you must always remember that death is not the end — only the beginning. We will all meet again!"

I swallowed hard and poured out my own heart. "Just look at what God has allowed us to see. The Vietnamese families in our home, now standing strong in spite of wars and separation. They are blessing people all over America. And just think about 'our boys' across the country and in foreign lands, standing true."

---

*We all live on the edge of eternity —
the beginning!*

Ralph gave us that whimsical smile of his. "If Lena were here, she'd sing her song, 'So many falling by the wayside. Please help them stand.' "

"And if Lena were with us today," I added, "she'd be calling out their names. Even the hippies, whose names we can't remember, are someplace — and Lena would be praying, 'God help them to stand.' "

"Well, Mom," Ralph mused, "I guess you never realized you would write six books in the eighties — and these books will stand. They're true stories of everyday living."

He brightened and added, "I think we should plan a big reunion by the sea. Do you realize that for twenty years we have stood? Not only that, but also all our children love God and want to serve Him. I think it's about time our children got together. Won't they have some stories to tell?"

Chris put on another pot of coffee; the children sat and listened. These were the stories of faith they would remember when other walls in their lives came tumbling down.

Although the miles separate us from the ones we love, our hearts never move. Dan and Virginia are on the West Coast. Jan and Jud, and their children, Heather and Chad, are on the New England Coast. Ralph and Chris, and their four children, Shawn, Eric, Sarah and Kathryn, are in the South. Harold and I, also in the South, hold them all close in our hearts and daily bring them all to the throne of grace.

Recently, I read a story of a brave woman who was determined to save a famous lighthouse. With the help of many people, she planted reed stems, and the wall stood. The slender reeds held the rain water, and, with its nourishment, grew tightly together, securing the lighthouse.

I thought of all the *reed stems,* the faithful people of God filled with the living water—planted by God and nourished by His living Word—standing together, united in faith in Jesus Christ.

The lashing winds of man's humanistic philosophy are driving against the cross of Jesus Christ, the light of the world—but the LIGHT will stand!

The *reed stems* stand. The cross stands. The ones we took in "as is" and God made "as His" still stand. Having done all, they still stand.

We all live on the edge of eternity—the beginning!

In the Cross of Christ [we] glory,
Towering o'er the wrecks of time.

I think I hear Keith singing, "Great is Thy Faithfulness, O God My Father . . ."

THE ALTAR

He came stooped — bent beneath his load,
And knelt before the altar there.
With broken heart and sorrow bowed,
He wept his lonely prayer.

The altar, new with shining wood,
Polished to reflect the grain,
Was splashed with tears — and stood
A symbol of healing from life's pain.

A step drew nearer to the form.
A hand reached out to touch.
"I'll kneel with you — take my arm.
Listen, God loves you much.

I made this altar — polished new,
With velvet stoop to kneel and pray.
The darkened wood of polished hue
Once was twisted, gnarled and grey.

I had two pieces of mahogany.
One was from the jungle warm,
Soft, porous, dark specks to see,
The tree grew fast — cut too soon.

The other sprang in mountains cold
With rocky soil — resisting power,
But the young tree grew firm and bold,
Stood strong and hard until this hour.

So often men in easy places
Grow porous in the soft ground.
The battles come. We miss their faces —
For in the fury, they turn around.

But then the trees in mountains high,
With winds that blow and roots so deep,
Are God's people who to Him draw nigh
And face the storms, knowing He will keep.

So I chose the tree, hard, tested grain,
Polished to reflect a glow.
See the white specks of rocky lime,
Strong—unbending 'neath sorrow's blow.

    I searched for another piece of wood,
    But the hardened tree had twisted and bent.
    And I threw it where the other scraps stood
    In a pile of castoffs, discarded and rent.

But the Master whispered, 'You are skilled
To take the twisted—rent and torn—
With your craftsman's hands turn at will
The bent and bruised to a piece reborn.'

    So I took in my hand the twisted wood,
    Planing and molding it into place.
    The Master craftsman understood
    The beauty of the bruised, saved by grace.

Then I searched for the velvet, royal blue,
To place on the kneeling pad to pray;
For we are royalty before this altar new
To receive God's grace—new for this day.

    Come, let the Master take your life
    And make the crooked places plain;
    The rough-marred life by sin and strife,
    In His dear name He can reclaim."

The two walked into the sunset hour
As the golden rays lit the church stained pane.
Chimes rang out from the steeple tower;
The Way of the Cross leads Home again.

—Dedicated to our son Ralph
Father's Day, June 19, 1977
Love, Mother